DIGNITY IN POLICING

How Emotional Well-Being Saves

Lives, Families, and Careers

D1526709

by

Marcel Brunel & Dan Newby

Emotional Autobiography in Five Short Chapters

Chapter 1.
I walk into a situation.
There is an emotion.
I fall into it. I am lost…I am confused.
I'm not at fault.
It takes forever to find a way out.

Chapter 2.
I walk into the same situation.
There is the emotion again.
I pretend I don't see it.
I fall into it again.
I can't believe I am back in the same place,
It's not my responsibility.
It still takes a long time to get out.

Chapter 3.
I walk into the exact situation again.
There it is the same emotion.
I see it there.
I still fall into it…it's a habit.
But my eyes are open. I know where I am.
It is my responsibility.
I find my way out.

Chapter 4.
I walk into the situation with new eyes.
There is the emotion.
I have a choice.
I walk around it.

Chapter 5.
I walk into the situation.
I choose a different emotion.

Based on the poem "Autobiography in Five Short Chapters" by Portia Nelson

There is no "I" without "we".

This book was inspired by and is dedicated to Susie Brunel and Lucy Núñez. They are our respective lights, muses, and guides in life and have contributed to this book in ways that they cannot imagine.

In gratitude,

Marcel and Dan

Contents

Advanced Praise..i

Preface..iv

Introduction...xxxiv

Section 1: Where We Are Today 1

Chapter 1: A Short History of Emotions in Policing.............2

Chapter 2: Policing and the Power of Perception 10

Chapter 3: Yes, and… 28

Chapter 4: "But wait! What are Emotions?"......................39

Section 2: What Has Been Missing.............................54

Chapter 5: Stop Looking out There….it is all in Here 55

Chapter 6: Right Decisions Require the Right Emotions.....65

Chapter 7: They're Called "Your Emotions" for a Reason ...80

Section 3: Program of Action 88

Chapter 8: Behaving our Way into Emotional Maturity 89

Chapter 9: Imposter Syndrome: Alive and Well in Policing 100

Chapter 10: Emotional Literacy is not Something you Believe in, it is Something you do. 109

Chapter 11: Successive Approximation 118

Chapter 12: Taking it to the Street 140

Chapter 13: Dignity, the Über Emotion 160

FAQs 168

Appendix A 174

Acknowledgments..176

Advanced Praise

"Dignity in Policing is as insightful and as real as it gets. This book will benefit every rank through the chain of command".

- Bill M., Police Chief

"The timing of this book couldn't be better to serve as a perfect resource and tool for emotional wellness".

- Brad F., Chief of Police

"This book is not just a "good read". It is a deep dive into an essential skill for 21st-century police officers".

- Rick R., Chaplain

"This book opens essential new horizons for law enforcement, transitioning the image of a stoic and emotionally stunted profession to one that is emotionally competent. Beyond a doubt, the authors' work is a game changer in the world of public safety and law enforcement".

- Brandy K., Professional Staff Manager

"In my opinion, Dignity in Policing is a must-read as it provides insight and a unique perspective into the emotional aspects of policing and provides a progressive approach and playbook for our officers to not just stay physically fit, but emotionally fit".

- Steve D., Chief of Police

"I have been in police work for ten years, and a detective for over half of that. This book is beyond helpful and goes deeper than Emotional Survival, it is *Emotional Living*".

- Ashley C., Detective

"This book can act as a comprehensive guide not just for enhancing emotional intelligence, but also for refining emotional literacy – the skill of identifying, labeling, and adeptly managing your emotions. Its benefits extend beyond the professional realm, and I believe it can make a positive impact on your personal life as well".

- Natalie N., Detention Officer

"I wholeheartedly believe the message in this book is an important one, we must first look internally to be able to understand what is occurring externally."

- Jalen R., F.T.O.

"If this book, Dignity in Policing, had been in my hands years ago it would have assisted me in the many leadership challenges I would face. We need to deal with our emotions first, so we can take care of others."

- Max T., LE Leadership Development Manager/Reserve Police Officer

"Dignity in Policing is a must-read for all of us with the responsibility of leadership positions. By recognizing and responding to the emotions of others, leaders can address issues more effectively, provide support when needed, and inspire teams to perform their best with true hearts for serving others".

- Bob M., Lieutenant

"This book is not only a practical guide to emotional intelligence, but it focuses on our police culture. The methods and theories make perfect sense and apply to all areas in law enforcement, from your rookie street cop to the Chief of Police.

- Beto B., Major

"Dignity in Policing" serves as a comprehensive guide, offering practical tools for emotional self-care, paving the way for officers to lead healthier, more fulfilling professional and personal lives. Its emphasis on dignity - a belief in inherent worth - becomes the guiding principle for officers, shaping their responses, actions, and relationships in both professional and personal spheres".

- Lindsay W., Mental Health Coordinator

"I always appreciated and valued the book "Emotional Survival for Law Enforcement". This book is the next step in first responder evolution. It is a key to improving all aspects of your life and making you more of an asset.

- Bill S., Officer

"This book dares us to look deeper at our inner selves so that we can push through the emotional blockages that operate to keep us all, including retirees, from embracing and enjoying the full range of our new, post-policing "now."

- Jacqueline S., Chief of Police (Retired)

Preface

Who are we?

Marcel and Dan are teachers, coaches, practitioners, and mindful human beings. Our goal is to be a spark for good, a pilot light, always there, ready and waiting to ignite a bigger flame. Our pasts can be broken down into two categories: before and after; what we were like before we became emotionally literate, and what we are like now.

Our shared purpose is to help others evolve emotionally and find the path that leads to their own emotional mastery. Our highest hope is that you will read these pages and come to realize that it is time to take a new look at your emotional understanding and competence.

I, Marcel, use my background in psychology every day. Over the past nine years, I've become a subject matter expert in first responder wellness by helping others see where I've stumbled and how my rock bottom became my rock bottom. When I got to despair, I decided to stop digging. In my marriage, I thought ignoring hard problems made those hard problems go away. Silence was my immature approach to manipulating others, regardless of whether they were right or wrong. In my career, I tried to think my way out of emotional situations.

Then, I realized that it is impossible to solve emotional problems intellectually. At that time in my life, emotional literacy was not even a rumor in my head, let alone an effective part of my personality. I had toughness wrong. Yelling and being callous towards others was not my best work. It has taken me years to learn that emotions come out of my mouth, and that toughness is really about my ability to create the time and space needed for making the most successful and appropriate choice under discomfort. Meaning, that sometimes it is important to display my emotions, and sometimes it serves me to delay expressing them.

While working closely with over 90 police agencies, from small departments with just fifteen first responders to large ones with thousands, I have a front-row seat observing the role emotions play during the entire first responders' journey. Since my journey began, I have studied the behaviors, stressors, and personalities of more than 4,000 first responders.

Clients describe the emotional challenges that begin in their first days at the academy, their first day on the job, or the moment an urgent call comes into dispatch and extends into the office of the chief of police. By working both 1:1 and in large groups with first responders, I help them acknowledge their experiences and build awareness of the impact emotions have in their lives and on their families and careers.

Most of the problems I see in agencies are relationship issues running around, masquerading as operational issues. When emotions become overextended, decision-making, problem-solving, and relationship-building suffer. For most, emotional literacy is learned in the laboratory of life when the stakes are high, emotions run strong, and opinions vary.

As an instructor with many police learning institutions, including the FBI National Academy, I can assure you that most first responders, from all parts of the world, struggle with recognizing and reconciling their emotions.

My journey is ongoing. I am a sober alcoholic and have danced on the edge of losing my family and myself. This happens when you are delusional because you do not recognize what is true. I will never graduate from the school of self-awareness. More will always be revealed to me. Remembering that my emotions are messengers, not dictators, is one area I easily forget. When I am not conscious of my emotions, I am at their mercy, and they can dictate my behavior for better or worse. I must continue to stay alert and remind myself daily that all emotions want to be acknowledged and experienced. I am still learning that if I am unable to forgive, then I will continue to go through the world, remembering only how I've been hurt.

My army background parallels the constantly changing, overly scrutinized, expected-to-be-perfect nature of policing. Being part of a scout platoon, where the sergeant showed favoritism, depleted my ambitions to stay in the army. Having a platoon leader micromanage me created resentment and self-doubt early in my life.

While actively engaged with a city leadership team, I discovered my true purpose—a commitment to help first responders navigate their current work emotions and to be more prepared emotionally when they retire.

It was during this period that I met Dan. I wanted first responders to experience how the work Dan does can create meaningful change in their mindset, skillset, and craft. Because you cannot give what you do not have, you have to start with yourself.

I, Dan, am a champion for emotional literacy. Discovering and developing emotional literacy has changed my life in positive and significant ways and has led to a deep desire to help others benefit from increased emotional understanding and growth.

In my late 30s and early 40s, I suffered from depression and addiction. Facing those taught me that although the visible aspects of these were behavioral, the driver was emotional. I was running from my emotions. They were scary and felt horrible, and I had no idea how to come to terms with them in any other way. So, I tried to avoid them by immersing myself in my addiction.

The despair of those experiences drove me to seek treatment, but they also led me to begin exploring my emotional ignorance and to look for a new way of understanding emotions. My search has led me to see emotions as logical, practical, and learnable, and my curiosity and desire to serve have been guiding me ever since.

I've learned to trust my emotions as a source of information. I've learned that emotions come and go and that noticing and naming them helps me use them to navigate my life. Intentionally including emotions in my decision-making produces better choices and the emotional agility I've learned helps me from getting stuck and blinding me to possibilities. Personally, I consider them an enormous gift.

I am a globally recognized subject matter expert on emotional literacy and the author of four books, including *The Field Guide to Emotions* and *The Unopened Gift: A Primer in Emotional Literacy*. My writing has been translated into Spanish, Italian, German, and Slovak. I am the founder of the School of Emotions, which offers courses in emotional literacy and its application. I am regularly invited to be a guest on a wide variety of platforms to share my practical approach to emotional learning and growth.

For six years, I led courses at the University of Calgary and now teach classes at the University of Wisconsin. I have consulted with school systems in Michigan on social-emotional learning curriculum and with a range of organizations around the world that are seeking to understand how to build and leverage emotional competence in their leaders and teams.

Important things in life do not always come with directions. When you got married or had your first child, you were not given a how-to manual. Marcel and I hope that the things we have learned will help you to see in new ways, like an updated pair of glasses.

What you will read in this book is not held up as "The Truth." We, the authors, offer our learning, experiences, insights, thoughts, and suggestions for your consideration. You will decide what is of value to you and what is not. Only embrace what you can to the extent you're ready. We hope you will challenge everything we are saying through the lens of openness and curiosity.

Having worked with people in different disciplines and a variety of backgrounds located in all parts of the world, we have discovered that we are all blind, just to different things. That opens the possibility that we can learn from one another.

Why did we write this book?

We wrote this book because we have something to say about emotions in policing. We hope we say it well, but we are not in the convincing business. If you believe emotions are not important, no explanation is needed. If you believe emotions are important, no explanation is necessary. So, are you permanently stuck if you believe emotions are not important? A bit, perhaps, because improving your well-being and interpersonal skills has little to do with intelligence, willpower, or perfection. It has everything to do with curiosity, honesty, boldness, sincerity, and humility, all emotions.

Many times, clients say to us, "I wish my colleagues could have heard your message." When it is appropriate, we suggest that maybe the message was meant for them. Building on this idea, we see this book as an emotional literacy roadmap. We give everyone who reads this book the right to be clumsy and sincere as you begin to apply our ideas and practical suggestions.

Our goal is to prioritize dignity in policing. The dignity of the profession and of those you serve. Dignity while improving police culture. Dignity, while enhancing a first responder's sense of identity, purpose, and significance that steers them towards continuing to do the next right thing, is our goal.

During our decades of work, we have witnessed firsthand the consequences of both addressing and neglecting emotional learning. In particular, we are struck by the power of understanding and elevating the emotion of dignity. When dignity is respected and strengthened, trust flourishes, relationships grow, and justice is sought with compassion.

When dignity is disregarded, fractures emerge between law enforcement and the communities they serve, which breeds skepticism, resentment, and a breakdown in social cohesion.

When first responders feel dignity, their willingness to disclose their mental health challenges increases, leading to early intervention, appropriate treatment, and the opportunity for healing and personal growth. By prioritizing dignity in law enforcement, we can effectively promote the overall mental wellness of first responders, ensuring their resilience and enhancing their ability to serve and protect their communities. Being fully armed and emotionally hijacked creates an environment in which a single negative incident can overshadow multiple positive accomplishments.

Another goal for this book is to help ensure that the best day you have ever had at your agency is one that is still out ahead of you. Improving ourselves is a balance between challenge and competence. This approach means that we stay ready, so we don't have to get ready; improvement as a choice, instead of a reaction. It is not our goal to fix you but to invite you to a broader view so that you have more possibilities to choose from. Our greatest hope is to provide insights and practices that help weave emotional literacy into your life, family, and career.

This book will help you be more principled, prepared, and skilled in working through your everyday challenges. In our work with first responders, we find that we are often outsiders with insider information. We are hoping that our experiences and learning will bring a new perspective to the work you do and the challenges you face.

Who did we write it for?

First and foremost, it is for you. Wherever you are and however you got there, this book can help you go further. We're not talking about 'moving up' in rank/title, we're talking about moving ahead in life in a way that fulfills and satisfies you. A life with less suffering and more balance. A life in which you feel empowered as the decision maker and confident the answers will come when your house is in order.

We also wrote this book for your loved ones and the communities you serve. Your emotions impact them more deeply than you may know. Each of us is defined by our relationships, and caring for them begins with our emotional competence.

From our work, we know that policing can be extremely highly challenging. You have chosen a role that often puts you between a "rock and a hard place." It isn't unusual to have conflicting or competing interests. You may feel it is a noble profession and that you are trustworthy, but you will encounter many people who do not share those opinions.

This book was written for everyone inside a police agency. As you read the paragraphs below, take in how an individual with your rank or title suggests leveraging this book. If the title or rank does not match yours exactly, maybe you'll find a message that resonates with you.

Accreditation and Compliance Specialists

Emotional intelligence and literacy are new and just-in-time paradigms being explored in law enforcement. Accreditation and Compliance Specialists play an important role in assisting agencies with either reinforcing culture and/or shaping new culture. Accreditation and Compliance focuses on assuring best practices and policies are achieved and contribute to the overall mission of the organization.

Emotional training, development, and reinforcement are critically important to the internal and external environment of law enforcement agencies. It is timely as it intersects with related topics such as de-escalation, Active Bystandership for Law Enforcement, and psychological safety. It provides professional staff and sworn law enforcement personnel with the ability to increase self-awareness reflection (know oneself) and then to effectively interact and intervene with internal and external stakeholders. When exercised appropriately, emotional skills can be a game changer in any law enforcement-related encounter or interaction. This book/topic truly opens an important new frontier for law enforcement. Looking forward to this new frontier...

Richard W., Accreditation and Compliance Specialist

Animal Control Lead Officers

Being an Animal Control Officer and walking into an animal hoarding house, showing up on a scene where a dog is still alive but has been shot multiple times, or you're told, "I took my eyes off him for only a second," and now the animal is at the bottom of the pool with no chance of resuscitation, you're hit all at once by emotions you can't show. "Suck it up, buttercup, it's part of the life that I chose to participate in," changes to "I can handle this and come out the other side less scathed because I was provided the training and tools to survive that moment."

Most Animal Control Officers hit burnout by year two, but if there was a focus on emotional well-being like there is on mental health, it could be a lifelong career for many more than just the few that survive the chaos. We all have to remember we do have value and add worth to our department, regardless of any awards or recognitions we may not receive. For me, chapter 9 reiterates this. Eventually, the impact overwhelms you, and not having the tools to handle the side effects can lead to a disastrous outcome. "Dignity in Policing" provides tools to navigate and control our emotional health while helping to increase our emotional literacy.

Corrina H., Animal Control Lead Officer

Assistant Chiefs

Dignity in Policing is a great reminder that we are all human. No matter how good an officer, detective, supervisor, assistant chief, or chief you are, a "just the facts" approach doesn't work. For thousands of years, our ancestors have had to quickly take in the facts of the moment and balance them against the emotions felt in the same moment. The big difference is that it is often easy to see the facts that are influencing the moment, like an approaching storm or a wrong-way driver. It is much harder to pinpoint the emotions present in the same moment that can influence a decision just as much or even more than the facts.

I got some very good advice from a mentor years ago that goes like this: "It is not what we don't know that gets us in a bind, it is often what we don't know that we don't know that bites us." Dignity in Policing helps us to see why and how we are influenced by our emotions and what we can do to dial up or down on the emotion needed in the moment to make the best decision. The unique thing about learning to deal with emotions is that the skills are just as relevant to the officer on the street dealing with a high-stress and dramatic call for service as they are for department leaders who experience similar emotions in their daily decisions that can impact the lives of officers and citizens. Just as the officer on the street's highest desire is to make the right decision in the moment, department leaders deal with emotional influence when making decisions concerning what is best for public safety in their respective cities.

In policing, just like in sports, we train at what we know we need to be good at. For example, we train our officers in how to write a good report and how to be proficient with a firearm, just like a quarterback trains to take a snap and throw a good pass. The same must hold true when it comes to handling emotions; if we want to be good at it, we must practice. As leaders, we must work to understand and practice the management of emotions to set a good example within our agencies. If we want our officers to be good at the emotional management process, we must first model that behavior, setting the tone for the department's culture. To conclude, I'll go back to the above sports analogy: after big plays and especially at the end of the game, the cameras always go to the coach; the coach sets the tone.

Neal B., Assistant Chief

Assistant Police Directors

Humans are emotional beings, and emotions are part of our humanity. Marcel and Dan describe our mission to better understand our emotions. In this timely book, they identify how properly aligned emotional literacy and emotional intelligence are the keys to better serving the people to whom public servants are accountable. This book offers smart, practical advice for building emotional competence

–and a guide to assist in emotional development to foster rewarding human change.

Rick R., Assistant Police Director

<u>Cadets</u>

Each person's progression through a career in law enforcement is unique on many levels. The one experience we all share is the transition from civilian to officer. You, as a Cadet, are facing a metamorphosis, unlike most in the professional arena. It has been a great privilege to hold a position that allows me to closely observe and actively participate in the evolution of hundreds of police cadets each year.

What I've learned through intensive, long-term interaction with police cadets is that successful transition has far less to do with one's cognitive abilities or skillset and much more to do with emotional development. Your goal should be to gain the necessary knowledge and skills without losing the very qualities and characteristics that make you you! The emotions that YOU feel when considering concepts such as Power, Trust, Justice, and Duty are what make you a rare and valuable asset to the Law Enforcement profession.

I challenge you to self-reflect with the "Gradually, and then Suddenly" concept from Chapter 1 in mind. All of your gradual growth and development into a police officer should not result in a sudden realization that you've left behind the person you were when you chose this profession. That realization rarely comes without damage to you, your loved ones, or the community around you. To the person just beginning their law enforcement career, *Dignity in Policing* serves as an invaluable tool to enhance your sense of self-agency and self-confidence when you need it most.

Jeremy S., Academy Cadet Officer

Captains

The emotional well-being of police captains is intricately linked to their emotional intelligence and emotional literacy. These vital skills enable them to navigate the complex and often emotionally charged situations they may encounter as a command staff member. Emotional intelligence and emotional literacy that Marcel and Dan speak to in this book equip you with the ability to understand your own emotions and also help foster positive relationships within your teams and communities. When you think back throughout your career, we all have those "bookmarks". These instances were either the highlight of your career or, in most cases, were a critical or traumatic event. How we survive those events is greatly determined by how emotionally "fit" we are. As leaders within a police department, we are responsible for being emotionally intelligent and literate to recognize the events that play out around us and be the strong leaders our teams deserve. I can't help but wonder how differently I would have handled those bookmarks in my career if I had been armed with the information in this book!

Jared L., Captain

Chaplains

I have served as a police chaplain for over 22 years. During that time, I have seen the toll that poorly regulated emotions can exact on the men and women of law enforcement. As Marcel and Dan point out in this book, emotions are not optional, how we respond to those emotions is. This book is not just a "good read". It is a deep dive into an essential skill for 21st-century police officers. The emotional toll of the job is well documented, and the results are what makes police officers the highest-rated group for heart disease, hypertension, and diabetes. It is what leads to a 200% greater likelihood of abusing alcohol and a divorce rate that is nearly twice the national average. And it is part of the reason that police officers have a life expectancy that is 22 years less than the general population. Officers interact daily with people in their worst moments. They are constantly under scrutiny from media and through the ubiquitous cell phone video footage of "cops gone wild". They, unlike most professions, live with the ever-increasing demands that the public places on the police while expecting them to never make a mistake or to respond in a less-than-calm and professional manner. All of that is what makes this book a must-read, especially for police chaplains.

WARNING: The contents of this book can save a career, can save a marriage, and may save a life.

Rick R., Chaplain

Chiefs of Police

'Dignity in Policing' spotlights the importance of 'Emotional Regulation.' Police departments are comprised of employees with varying degrees of inherent emotional intelligence. Just as we learn through reading and writing to obtain linguistic literacy, we must also learn to develop our emotional literacy. Emotional wisdom and mastery emerge as we increase our ability to understand and regulate our emotions when and as we choose. As a profession, I believe it is important we begin to address the importance of each person's emotional competence, as it relates to each person's behavior. As Marcel and Dan state, "When I am not conscious of my emotions, I am at their mercy, and they can dictate my behavior for better or worse." This book can arm the brand new rookie with an awareness and tools to be mindful of as they enter our profession and further develop throughout their career. They'll be ahead of the game. It can provide current and future supervisors a resource & guide to lead their departments by sharing and cultivating their agency's emotional literacy. It can provide a departmental cultural standard & expectation through required promotional reading of the intentionality by a Chief to increase their department's overall emotional competence. Many departments are pursuing departmental wellness programs to improve all aspects of their employees' overall wellness: financial, mental, physical, spiritual, and emotional. The timing of this book couldn't be better to serve as a perfect resource and tool for emotional wellness in furtherance of that goal.

Becoming aware carries with it a responsibility to determine how you will act. It does not automatically make you responsible to fix it, but you can no longer ignore that you have a choice to make.

Brad F., Chief of Police

City Managers/Former Chiefs

I have been a public servant for almost 40 years with 35 of those serving as a police officer and police chief and the other five as a deputy city manager and city manager. When I began my career in 1984, the policing profession had not yet become fully aware and knowledgeable of the importance of officer wellness. Instead, the day-to-day stressors of police work were typically addressed through a culture of machoism and a belief that we were somehow tough enough to persevere through these human challenges without awareness or an understanding of how these emotions would often derail us into substance abuse, divorce, poor work performance, increased uses of force, fractured personal relationships, or even suicide. Over the years, police work has become even more challenging with officers now expected to handle many social issues such as mental health, unemployment, poverty, and homelessness. As a result, the mental health of our police officers is more taxed than ever as the job is more complex and demanding than ever before.

In my opinion, Dignity in Policing is a must-read as it provides insight and a unique perspective into the emotional aspect of policing and provides a progressive approach and playbook for our officers to not just stay physically fit, but emotionally fit. As we've seen in high-profile incidents across the country and, as leaders have observed far too many times in disciplinary cases, our police officers must be whole and healthy to best serve our communities. Dignity in Policing is our opportunity, and quite frankly our responsibility, to provide this critical insight and expert guidance to ensure we are taking care of the men and women in blue who are performing the toughest job in America.

Steve D., City Manager/Former Chief

<u>Commanders</u>

As a commander, you have influence. You have influence not only in the operations of your agency, but more importantly, you have influence in the lives of those women and men you work with. Many of them look up to you, and some even want to achieve the rank you hold. For this and many other reasons, it is vital that you don't take your role lightly.

Conversations where you share your experience, successes, and struggles don't have to be formal. In fact, in my years of serving as a commander, it is the informal conversations that occur organically that are of the most value to others. These conversations can occur in the break room, while passing in the hallway, parking lot, or even in the gym.

As a commander, for you to be successful in your coaching and mentoring of others, you'll need to be vulnerable. Restated, you need to be honest with yourself, become emotionally literate, regulate your emotions, and be vulnerable enough to share with others how you got to where you are today.

If your journey has been like mine, it has been full of ups and downs. I have learned more from my mistakes than my successes. I know that the value of those hard-learned lessons is multiplied when I share with others so they don't repeat my mistakes.

Remember, you're a success story, but your story is only as good as the legacy you leave. The choice is yours.

Vernell D., Commander

Corporals

Dignity in Policing reminds us of the value and importance of mastering one's emotions while teaching us techniques to achieve this mastery. It encourages the reader to take this journey not because it is easy, but because it is important. Because as public servants in the field of law enforcement, we give ourselves to our community. We are tasked with caring for people. Caring about people. And that dedication takes a toll. As a Corporal, a first-line supervisor to officers making these sacrifices, we see the effects this selflessness has on a person, both personally and professionally. With the lessons learned in this book, Corporals can help those they supervise care for their emotions and themselves. They can recognize someone struggling and intercede, or identify an opportunity for growth, and in doing so counter the stigma that emotional awareness and expression has in the field of policing. By teaching officers that it's safe to be themselves, to be human, one can change a shift, a department, and eventually, a profession.

Jonathon K., Corporal

Detectives

I have been in police work for ten years, and a detective for over half of that. This book is beyond helpful and goes deeper than Emotional Survival; it is *Emotional living*. Police work can leave one jaded, and investigative work takes its toll on all of us at some point. Applying these new tools has assisted me personally with proper contribution to my colleagues during tough scenes, with the victim's family, and with the community that I serve.

Take away from this book one thing – you don't have to be an emotional teenager, but acknowledging and applying your own self-discovery with what you feel and what is a "trigger" can help you overcome the outside noise of police work. If this was applied in a police culture aspect, departments would be investing in their people both in-house and out. I can only find the truth as an investigator by making a connection with those who have the information, I need to solve my cases, and connections are made when a person feels they are emotionally safe with me. Would I be safe with myself? After reading Dignity in Policing, the answer is Yes! Learn to feel and be okay with your emotions, they aren't permanent, and you can overcome the tough ones – if you want to.

Ashley C., Detective

Deputy Chiefs

The pressures attached to the rank of deputy chief are many. Stress at both work and home assumed shapes I never knew existed. Recognizing how I dealt with those stressors and how emotions played into them made me aware of the need for healthy ways of dealing with them. One of the biggest issues I personally faced once I became a deputy chief was the realization of how many things I didn't. This book helped me understand how to recognize my own defensiveness and find ways to be more open to learning by embracing connections and being present in the moment. Intentionality is the key word I found to be the vessel for deliberate connection with others instead of self-protection when I am facing uncertainty. Seeing things in that light has made a difference in both my professional and personal relationships.

Timothy V., Deputy Chief

Detention Managers

Throughout my professional journey, I've been in the position of police officer, detention officer, and now as a regional holding facility manager. In my roles as a police officer and a detention officer, I learned the importance of managing my emotions when dealing with citizens, handling specific calls, and even in my personal life at home after a long day at work. While each role presented its own unique set of challenges, both fields contributed significantly to the development of my emotional intelligence.

As a recently appointed manager and leader in a detention facility, this book can act as a comprehensive guide not just for enhancing emotional intelligence, but also for refining emotional literacy – the skill of identifying, labeling, and adeptly managing your emotions. Its benefits extend beyond the professional realm, and I believe it can make a positive impact on your personal life as well.

Natalie N., Detention Manager

FTOs, SWAT, Patrol, and Fitness

I have worked in Law Enforcement for 8 years in different roles, including Jailer, Officer, Field Training Officer, and SWAT Operator. As a Field Training Officer, I am constantly looking for ways to better facilitate learning for trainees and myself. I wholeheartedly believe the message in this book is an important one; we must first look internally to be able to understand what is occurring externally. The lessons learned from this roadmap can help improve the quality of training for trainees, leading to an improvement in a department's overall culture. The book sheds a light on wellness and how self-reflection is critical to the change sought after. After reading the book, I have a better awareness of how I feel, and how I can navigate those feelings to be more accountable in my role. We can't control how we feel, but we can have a better understanding on how to react to our emotions. In order to improve our profession, we must start with ourselves; this book helps us find that path.

Jalen R., F.T.O.

Leadership Development Managers

I have served as a full-time law enforcement officer for 11 years, and after learning about emotional intelligence, I wish I had known about it at the beginning of my career. I now serve as a reserve police officer and the leadership development manager at the Bill Blackwood Law Enforcement Management Institute of Texas. My role currently is extremely relevant to assisting in providing curriculum.

This book, Dignity in Policing, if in my hands years ago would have assisted me in the many leadership challenges I would face. While reading this book, I recalled being promoted young in my career as a Sergeant (20s) and a Lieutenant (30s) and recalled the many days of anxiety, doubt, and worry due to the role and profession. These emotions negatively affected not only my work life but my home life as well.

The practical application given in this book is that having emotional intelligence as a part of professional development is paramount in the roles of leaders like me. In training, there must be intentional comprehensive training for first responders in relation to emotional intelligence. The training must include working sessions, simulations, and scenario-based training to enhance self-awareness, empathy, emotional regulation, and communication skills. This message must continuously be shared with law enforcement leaders in mandated training and leadership development courses around the nation.

This book reinforces the need for law enforcement leaders to provide quality level emotional intelligence training so careers, marriages, and relationships can be healthy. Leaders must challenge the law enforcement profession to "Stop looking out there….it's all in here…" (Chapter 5, Dignity in Policing). We need to deal with our emotions first, so we can take care of others."

Max T., LE Leadership Development Manager/Reserve Police Officer

Lieutenants

Looking back over three decades in public service, with the past 27 years being in law enforcement, one major thing that stands out to me is that many of our organizations have really fallen behind in focusing on the internal development of personnel.

We put emphasis on community programs, accountability, oversight, equity, recruitment, and hiring, but often at the expense of coaching, mentoring, career planning, team building, retention, and individual development. As lieutenants, we are in prime positions to help front-line supervisors cultivate and develop true servant-leader and people-first mindsets.

Emotional intelligence is a critical attribute for leaders because it enables us to build stronger connections with our teams and make more effective decisions. When we understand our own emotions, we are able to remain composed in high-pressure situations, make rational choices, and create a positive culture that values integrity, continuous improvement, and transparency. This, in turn, encourages front-line supervisors to adopt similar values and behaviors, ultimately leading to a more accountable and resilient police force dedicated not only to public safety and crime-fighting but also to the ethical principles that form the foundation of a just society.

We've all heard some form of the statement, "Take care of the people, and they'll take care of the mission." Emotional intelligence is the foundation of effective leadership, enabling leaders to navigate the complex challenges we face every day in law enforcement with authenticity, empathy, and resilience. Dignity in Policing is a must-read for all of us with the responsibility of leadership positions. By recognizing and responding to the emotions of others, leaders can address issues more effectively, provide support when needed, and inspire teams to perform their best with true hearts for serving others.

Bob M., Lieutenant

<u>Majors</u>

I have been a police officer for 25 years and loved every minute of my career. I was born to do the job and cannot imagine doing anything else. I have learned a lot throughout my career but gained the most knowledge after I became a supervisor. Effective leadership is incredibly important in law enforcement and can be the difference between being successful or just drawing a paycheck. I read about the term "emotional intelligence" when I was first promoted to lieutenant, and I embraced the effectiveness of its concepts and strategies. The ability to recognize and manage your own emotions is a game-changer when leading people. Once you are proficient with that, it is your responsibility to recognize others' emotions, so you can better help, encourage, guide, support, and lead them.

We all have our own personality traits and character flaws we must live with, but when you treat everyone with kindness, dignity, and respect, and use a Servant Leader approach, you will be very effective no matter what your rank or assignment is. This book is not only a practical guide to emotional intelligence, but it focuses on our police culture. The methods and theories make perfect sense and apply to all areas in law enforcement, from your rookie street cop to the Chief of Police.

Whether you are communicating with someone in crisis at a domestic call, or giving a speech to your City Council, your emotional quotient will be much more useful than your intelligence quotient. Cops don't want leaders who think they know everything; cops want leaders who care about them and want them to thrive. The authors of this book give you the blueprint to help master your leadership skills, not only at work but also at home. It is tough to argue with the logic and reason expressed inside this book, and you will be a much better human being once you look in the mirror and perfect your skills in emotional literacy.

Beto B., Major

Mental Health Coordinators

From my perspective as a Wellness Manager within law enforcement, the primary message of "Dignity in Policing" revolves around emotional self-care and the importance of nurturing the emotional well-being of officers. This book emphasizes that emotions have always been integral to policing and that every short-term behavior holds long-term consequences. Dan and Marcel underscore the need for officers to recognize the power of emotions, highlighting that emotions are a core competency and life skill, far from being a weakness. As a Wellness Officer, this book resonates deeply as it delves into emotional regulation versus suppression. It emphasizes that emotional regulation, when officers acknowledge, understand, and modulate their emotions in a balanced manner, is crucial for maintaining emotional well-being and fostering genuine connections - vital elements for effective policing and personal health.

The book provides valuable context for the culture within law enforcement agencies and its impact on officer wellness. It outlines how the brain functions in dealing with emotions, exploring denial and suppression as hindrances to emotional health. It differentiates emotional suppression from regulation, underlining the adverse effects of habitual suppression on stress levels and interpersonal relationships. The book stresses that emotional self-care is an ongoing process akin to breathing, requiring continuous attention, reflection, and resolution of emotions in real-time.

Reading this book provided a profound insight—emotional well-being is fundamental and cannot be achieved solely through mental health support. Instead, it's about emotional capacity, understanding, and regulating emotions. I'd strongly recommend this to my peers because it presents a roadmap to develop emotional competencies vital for officers' resilience and effectiveness in handling challenges.

This book's value to our profession is immense. It highlights emotional well-being as foundational for officers' mental health, showing how emotions significantly impact mental health and functionality. It demystifies mental health, emphasizing the need to embrace emotions to build resilience and navigate life's stresses effectively. "Dignity in Policing" serves as a comprehensive guide, offering practical tools for emotional self-care, paving the way for officers to lead healthier, more fulfilling professional and personal lives. Its emphasis on dignity—a belief in inherent worth—becomes the guiding principle for officers, shaping their responses, actions, and relationships in both professional and personal spheres.

Lindsay W., Mental Health Coordinator

__Officers__

I have worked in law enforcement for twelve years and have held several different positions including patrol, bicycle patrol, and community services. Whether you are new to the law enforcement profession, a long-time veteran, or even retired, this book has something to offer you. The authors want to show you how you can recognize, regulate, and use your emotions to your advantage, rather than allowing them to control you or be a stumbling block to your life and career. I was shocked to learn that emotions are normal, useful, and are not your enemy.

I have spent a lot of time in my life suppressing my emotions, refusing to acknowledge them, and then living with the negative consequences. No more. With the material in this book, I am learning. I am growing. I am evolving. I am no longer a slave to my emotions. I can now recognize my igniters and choose a different path. If you want to be a better person, a better officer, a better asset to your department and community, you need to read this book and take it to heart.

I always appreciated and valued the book Emotional Survival for Law Enforcement. This book is the next step in first responder evolution. It is a key to improving all aspects of your life and making you more of an asset.

Bill S., Officer

Professional Staff Supervisors

As a Manager over Professional Staff within a Police Department, I deeply appreciate the profound insights offered in this book. The authors address the critical and often overlooked aspect of law enforcement - the emotional intelligence of our leaders and professional staff. In a profession characterized by high stress, quick decisions, and public scrutiny, honing emotional skills can dramatically influence performance and overall well-being.

Emotional intelligence plays a pivotal role in effective job performance of a leader, especially in public safety careers where stress levels are high, and empathy is paramount. Being emotionally literate allows these essential professionals to navigate, manage, and understand their own emotions and those of others. It empowers us to self-assess our emotional state in real-time and adjust our responses accordingly. This understanding can help mitigate emotional responses that could impede decision-making.

I have seen the proof that fostering emotional literacy can significantly influence employee retention for myself and my staff. Many professional staff struggle with stress and subsequent burnout due to the intense emotional demands of the role. However, with a better grasp of emotional intelligence, these professionals can cope more effectively with stress, reduce professional burnout, and demonstrate better resiliency.

This book opens essential new horizons for law enforcement, transitioning the image of a stoic and emotionally stunted profession to one that is emotionally competent. Beyond a doubt, the authors' work is a game changer in the world of public safety and law enforcement.

Brandy K., Professional Staff Manager

Property Room/CID Files

Law enforcement personnel continually make high-risk decisions in trying situations. The way those decisions can affect emotions is very telling. It may be the high of saving a life or the low of informing a loved one with devastating news. The importance of empathy is that it allows all of us to better understand and relate to one another through our emotions. This book helps demonstrate the levels of emotions and how they intermingle with all aspects of law enforcement. Finding ways to manage the stressors that come with this job is essential for your health and well-being. I truly believe there is no harder profession out there and it just continues to be every day.

Lisa M., Property Room/CID Files

Retired Police Chiefs

I retired from law enforcement after a 37-year career, the last 11 of which were in service as a police chief. When I stepped into the top leadership position, like many executives, I very much appreciated conversations, books, and seminars addressing principles of leadership, the search for meaning, emotional survival, and emotional intelligence. As I neared retirement, I would have liked something similar but differently focused.

This book, *Dignity in Policing*, would have provided what I was looking for - the ability to recognize, understand, and put into perspective the cause of my anxieties about who I was going to be in retirement. I found *Dignity in Policing* to be impactful because it required a look back and a look ahead. My retirement from a career that at times was exceedingly challenging, somewhat exciting, always rewarding, and very meaningful, resulted in a sense of deflation, loss, and a bit of anxiety. I questioned my value, my purpose, and the origin of those two things.

The nature of these questions put me in an unfamiliar place, on uneven ground. Where I was typically so self-assured, measured, certain, and intentional in the workplace, with retirement, I was no longer any of those things. I was literally and figuratively in a new space. I found value in this book because it applies whether one is at the beginning of a career trajectory, is mid-career, or as was the case with me, post-career.

This book pointed out that it is a normal emotional reaction to engage in this questioning of a new existence, value, and purpose. Moreover, doing so within the framework of intentional, consistent, and purposeful action, buttressed by an understanding of self, is a function of emotional health and well-being. And given what the actuaries say about the post-career longevity for law enforcement members, *Dignity in Policing* provides important reminders and tools for understanding and managing the emotional self–the self that wants us to focus on our anxieties so much so that emotional peace becomes elusive. Because this emotional peace contributes to longevity, it must be nurtured. This book dares us to look deeper at our inner selves so that we can push through the emotional blockages that operate to keep us all, including retirees, from embracing and enjoying the full range of our new, post-policing "now."

Jacqueline S., Chief of Police (Retired)

Sergeants

Through my 23+ years in law enforcement, I have served in almost every aspect there is, including being a sergeant for over 8 years. In the beginning, we were taught to be strong, fearless officers, and not to show our feelings. But, as the authors put it, "There is a knife to your (our) throat, and you (we) are holding it."

Luckily, law enforcement has taken a turn, and we are becoming more human. However, suicide numbers amongst law enforcement are too high. As a supervisor, not only do we need to manage our own emotional wellness, but we must assist those that we supervise with managing theirs. It is our job to ensure they are protecting themselves, their loved ones, and the communities that we represent.

'Dignity in Policing' has many topics that can not only assist the officer but can help you with yourself and your team. A particular point is "An unaware person is dangerous." If an officer doesn't know, then they can't change it. This is where a supervisor needs to step in and help them become aware: Self-awareness + Others Awareness = Intentionality! It is crucial that we continue to train and learn about our emotional intelligence and literacy, and this book can be a good start, reminder, or talking point.

Walter L., Sergeant

Telecommunicators

I have been in Public Safety Communications for 13 years. I started as a line-level dispatcher and worked my way up through different roles to my current position as a Communications Manager. In our line of work, we tend to see the worst in people, and in turn, we can become negative over time, always looking for the dark side of things versus the good. This bleeds from our professional lives into our personal lives if we are not careful. This book, Dignity in Policing, teaches us how to reset ourselves and change our thinking. Change starts within us and that begins when we accept where we need to make those changes. It also teaches that it's okay to have emotions; we are, after all, human. After reading this, you will have the tools to navigate through your emotions and, in turn, become a stronger person that your team will feel safe with.

Amber S., Communications Manager

So, why are you in policing? How did you get here? Whatever rational explanations jump to mind, we propose that there is one or more emotions that shaped and drove your choice.

- Let's say you come from a family of first responders. The emotion that moved you to also become one might have been *loyalty* to tradition, *respect* you learned as a child, or *obligation* because you believed it was expected of you.

- Or perhaps you thrive on helping people who are in difficult situations. In that case, the emotion that drove your choice might be *satisfaction, pride,* or *compassion.*

- And then again, maybe it was work you fell into without planning, and your path was defined by *complacency, surprise,* or *acceptance.*

What is at stake?

The pressures of policing lead many first responders step by small step to self-destruction. There is a knife to your throat, and you are holding it. First responders are their own biggest threat. More officers take their own lives than are killed by other hands.

It is a sad fact that first responders are more likely to die from suicide than in the line of duty. In the U.S. in 2020, 116 first responders died by suicide, while 113 died in the line of duty (Stanton, 2022). In 2021, that number rose to 150 officers dying by suicide (Leone, 2022). Tragically, law enforcement officers have a 54% increase in suicide risk when compared to the civilian population (McAward, 2022). The problem seems to be even worse in smaller departments, which may not have an extensive support system or peer support resources.

First responders are also their own biggest jailers. They see and experience trauma and hold onto it for extended periods, yet they are responsible for their behavior regardless of what they are feeling. No one raised their hand in 4th grade and said that they wanted to grow up to have a job where other people did not have to fight fair even when you do and that when you retire, your life expectancy could be as short as 18 months.

Emotional literacy is for those who need it and want it. You can take out the words emotional literacy and put in the word sobriety. Sobriety is for those who need it and want it. Here is the key. Sometimes, in order to have something we have never had, we have to do some things we have never done. We hope this book can be the difference that makes that difference in your self-awareness and others-awareness, and how you show up in challenging situations.

Who you are in your role has tremendous impact. When you suffer, others suffer. When you thrive, others thrive. It is as simple as that.

We also wrote this book for your loved ones and the communities you serve. Each of us is defined by our relationships. If you say you are a father, it is because you have children, a partner, it is because you have a husband or wife, a leader, it is because you are trusted and respected by your followers, and for a first responder, it is because there is a community you serve. There is no 'I' without 'we'.

Introduction

<u>The six big ideas we're proposing</u>

1. **There is an ironclad connection between your emotions and the quality of policing that you deliver:** Understanding that relationship and building emotional competence leads to new approaches that serve all parties. Culture and wellness are interdependent and must become a national priority. Wellness is not a program. It is an agency decision that starts with how first responders are treated and begins with effective leadership. This can also be called trauma-informed leadership. It means that you, as a leader, must see each employee's circumstances through the lens of trauma by recognizing that most officers will experience more than 180 critical incidents in their careers.

2. **Emotional competence requires regularity and commitment:** It is not complex. It is not academic. It is not touchy-feely. It *is* important, and it changes lives, yours included, but it must be continually refreshed and practiced.

3. **Emotions are logical, learnable, and practical:** This is not how most grew up thinking about emotions, but we could.

4. **Emotional literacy is the tool that allows you to leverage the power of your emotional intelligence, just as reading, writing, and a robust vocabulary help you use your intellect:** Knowing "about" emotions is one thing; understanding them and knowing how to leverage them is another.

5. **Emotional agility allows you to regulate your behavior to address situations as they occur and is a skill you can**

learn: If you want to modify your behaviors, begin with mastering your emotions.

6. **The emotion that determines the regard with which you hold yourself is dignity:** In dignity, you believe, without question, that you are inherently worthy regardless of what others think or say. Sure, what others think of you matters, but what you think about yourselves matters more. That mindset opens the door to a world of possibilities.

The Microscope and the Mirror

People open a book for a variety of reasons. You may be here because you are curious about the link we see between dignity and policing. You may be skeptical that one emotion, like dignity, could generate much difference. You may be reading this book to see yourself better because:

- Personal development has always been part of your journey, and emotional literacy is something that you are seeking to learn more about.

- Your tank is full to overflowing, and you need relief from the pressure. When it comes to wellness, the higher you are on the department org chart, the harder it is to bring it up because you're supposed to be an icon as it relates to the operation. You try to be a Superhero in the equation as it relates to pushing through, but then all the people around you begin to suffer.

- You think it might provide insights and techniques to help you navigate the challenges of your roles while maintaining your own well-being and giving you the tools to support the well-being of those around you.

- You were given it as part of your police academy experience.

- You received a copy of it from your chief and were told to read it for an upcoming command staff retreat.

- You want to be promoted within your agency, and part of the promotion process is a list of books to read that you will be asked about during oral boards, and this book was on the reading list.

- Someone on your team described you as a bully or hardheaded.

- You were told you "must" read this book and are looking to try poking holes in our ideas.

- Maybe you are the Wellness Officer within your department or are part of a Crisis Intervention Team (CIT) and have been looking for 'beyond the obvious' approaches to agency culture and first responder wellness.

- You just transferred into another agency and were asked to read this book because the chief feels that this book is in alignment with their current thinking.

- And any of the other dozens of reasons is valid.

Whatever brought you here, we invite you to take a look and be curious about what we are suggesting.

Every year, we, the authors, have multiple opportunities to be in classrooms, coaching others through their emotional intelligence assessment results. We are keenly aware that there are different states of mind for learning. The four biggest ones we have worked with are IKE, Prisoner, Vacationer, and Learner. One or more may show up for you while reading this book.

IKE (I Know Everything):

- This is the person who wants to make sure we know how smart they are. They have seen it all and done it all. They believe first responders learn better from other first responders and not outsiders. IKEs believe that when leadership becomes emotionally literate, they will also automatically become emotionally literate. An IKE is often the first responder that quit but never left. Maybe you have a colleague, neighbor, or relative who is an IKE.

- The not-so-good news for IKEs is that they are blind but are not aware of it. They are "post-peak" because the best day they'll ever have is one they've already lived.

- IKEs may feel stuck in the policing profession. They feel the heat, and yet they can't see the light because they still have a couple of years to go till they retire. Just because you have been in policing for 25 years does not mean that you grew in knowledge along the way. Do you have 25 years in policing or 1 year in policing 25 times? Longevity does not equal competency.

- IKEs display emotions like *arrogance, denial, contempt, or entitlement* without even knowing it.

The Prisoner:

- The Prisoner is the person who does not want to be where they are. They believe they don't have a choice. They were told to show up, so they did, physically, at least.

- They are addicted to distractions. Prisoners have their phones up and are not concerned if it is distracting to others. They come in late from breaks and sneak out early.

- The not-so-good news for the Prisoner is that they are usually so busy doing trivial things they have no time for the vital few. Learning for a Prisoner is important and yet they feel it is not as valuable as what they are currently engaged in. The issue is not being busy; the issue is believing that activity equals productivity.

- Prisoners are typically the ones who say at the break that what they are learning is BS and that they have other things to be doing. They show up to class displaying emotions like *urgency, obligation, skepticism,* or *boredom.*

The Vacationer:

- This is typically the person who shows up with no idea what they are expected to accomplish during the session. They get to see their colleagues and maybe snag a free breakfast or lunch as a bonus.

- They are grateful and kind because they know it beats being at work and there is free food, but what the Vacationer never fully understands is that, just like water heated to 211 F, they may be one degree away from something that will transform their lives.

- They are sometimes called a "hanger" because the uniform just hangs on them. They want the recognition of a first responder without the effort.

- The Vacationer goes through life in *complacency*, *naivete*, or even *laziness*.

The Learner:

- The Learner is the student who realizes they are in school every day of their life. They're happy to be a beginner, a bit "clumsy, but trying", as they practice new skills, techniques, and approaches. Repetition strengthens and confirms they are learning. They realize the brain grows the most each time we make a mistake or struggle to understand.

- They're aware when they are pushed slightly off-center and thus are on the lookout for new ways to fluidly rebalance.

- The learner knows that putting down the microscope (examination of others) and picking up a mirror (examination of self) is a rewarding and healthy thing to do because you cannot influence what you cannot see.

- Learners are not embarrassed by their emotions. They know emotions are part of what makes them human. They know that striving for emotionlessness does not help manage challenging emotions.

- Learners show up with emotions like *humility, courage, curiosity*, and *sincerity*.

In our lifetimes as students, we, the authors, have been the IKE, Prisoner, Vacationer, and Learner. Our evolution to consistently show up as Learners has been one of successive approximation, getting better step-by-step over time. The microscope and mirror are two good tools for evaluation and evolution. Sometimes, we need to see the detail to understand what we are experiencing, and other times, we just need to see how we are showing up in the world.

As you read this book...

We invite you to read this book, keeping curiosity handy and knowing that the coming pages are suggestions only. No one can force you to "want to." We can't want you to be more emotionally literate than you want to be. We can only be a 49% shareholder in your success.

The growth of emotional literacy is already happening in policing. Those who embrace it can be tactical and tactful at the same time. Arrests can increase while citizen complaints go down. Emotional literacy enhances your competence with both the mirror and the microscope. It is yours for the taking if you so choose.

- We're asking you to look inward rather than outward because it is the invisible in you that makes the visible difference. People will always see on the outside what exists on the inside.

- We are not you. Only you can determine the value of what you read and whether or not to embrace it as your own. Own where you are. False bravado won't work. You can take the easy route and lower the bar or put in the extra effort to raise the floor.

- Leadership (Emotional Quotient) EQ is a learned ability that allows you to generate the emotions required for the task at hand. When you are a leader who does not do this well, it reveals itself as a lack of competence.

- Logic alone can never work as the basis for decision-making. When you think about which home to buy, which person to marry, or whether you can trust somebody, making your best choice requires emotional self-knowledge and emotional wisdom.

- Policies, oversight, and agency restrictions are needed, and yet the vast majority of a first responder's work is done independently and outside the immediate oversight of a supervisor. That means that many things you need must be done by you, like learning to effectively manage and respond to emotional experiences. No organization can learn that for you.

- This book was written post-Covid, George Floyd, and Tyre Nichols. We can all agree that these three traumatic events have changed policing. This book acknowledges the significant impact that they have had on our society, specifically on the field of policing. We believe that they point to the need for all of us to up our game in the area of emotional competency.

Some of the ideas or practices we suggest may feel awkward or uncomfortable for you. Even though they may not feel natural, hopefully, you will see that they are still worthwhile. We are not telling you this is going to be easy. We are ensuring you that it's going to be worthwhile. It may not be comfortable to tell someone we are sorry, yet it is often worthwhile. It may not be comfortable to have 15 energetic children at your home to celebrate your child's birthday, yet it may be worthwhile.

How to get the most out of this book...

At the end of each chapter, you'll find **Questions to ask yourself**. These are designed to help you make the reading relevant to you. They are also an attempt to get you to look inside and discover what you may not be aware of about your relationship with emotions.

You will also find a section called **Learning while performing**. Until emotions are put into practice, they are just a theory, a nice idea. Embodying emotions and truly understanding them comes through practice. Nothing is fully learned until it is fully applied.

And you'll find a **FAQ** section at the end of the book that gives answers to the questions we hear most often from our clients.

Terminology

Definitions you may find useful as you read:

- **Emotions:** The definition we use is that they are the "energy that moves us." This comes directly from the original word in Latin *emovere*, "that that moves us."

- **Emotional literacy (EL):** Understanding emotional fundamentals and being able to apply them in daily life. Analogous to linguistic literacy.

- **Emotional intelligence (EI):** The learned ability to navigate the emotions of self and others effectively so that we can appropriately match responses to situations.

- **Emotional quotient (EQ):** the level of a person's emotional intelligence, often represented by a score from a standardized test.

- **Leadership EQ:** The learned ability to generate the emotions needed to accomplish the task at hand.

- **Maturity:** The capacity to suffer well.

- **Emotional agility:** The ability to fluidly adapt emotionally to changing situations.

- **Emotional regulation:** The ability to choose the emotion and intensity of that emotion that serves best.

- **Emotional competence:** The knowledge of emotions demonstrated in your actions.

- **Emotional resilience:** the ability to bounce back from surprises or emotionally challenging situations.

Section 1:
Where We Are Today

Chapter 1
A Short History of Emotions in Policing

"Gradually, and then suddenly."

Chapter bullets

- Emotions have always been part of policing.
- Every short-term behavior has a long-term consequence.
- Fear and faith carpool together. You decide who is driving.
- It is the invisible that drives the visible.

Story

"Maybe some of you reading this book remember the world of policing over three decades ago, a time when the 1990s reigned supreme. If you do not, picture a landscape vastly different from the one we navigate today. Back then, emotions were considered as out of place as a cat in a dog park - especially in conversations among fellow first responders.

During those days, keeping a stiff upper lip was the unwritten rule. We were expected to suppress our emotions, to conceal any hint of vulnerability beneath a façade of unyielding strength. Feelings? Well, they were more like contraband than anything else. Our focus was on discussing financial strategies for retirement, while the notion of emotional well-being remained largely uncharted territory.

The concept of cameras monitoring our every move was a distant reality back then. The era of body-worn cameras and universal smartphones recording our interactions had yet to materialize. Our actions existed as fleeting moments, preserved only in the memories of those who bore witness. The thought of our deeds being subject to continuous scrutiny was beyond imagination.

Communication skills, in those days, were far from a focal point. Our training emphasized legal know-how and self-defense techniques, but the art of genuine engagement with the community was sidelined. The idea of extending a handshake to strangers? Almost laughable. We were indoctrinated with the principle of "officer safety," which discouraged familiarity with the very citizens we were sworn to protect.

As time marched forward, seismic shifts occurred - both technologically and culturally. The days of anonymous actions were replaced by the watchful gaze of body cameras and the always-present smartphones. Our deeds, once forgotten, were now etched into the digital fabric of reality.

Yet, this transformation wasn't just about gadgets and gizmos. It was about us, about how we adapted to the changing world. The mandate evolved from being mere enforcers of the law to becoming community-oriented champions. The motto shifted to "Serve and protect, with empathy and dignity." We found ourselves navigating the delicate balance between authoritative enforcement and compassionate understanding.

An intriguing paradox emerged. How to "be human without acting human?" This challenge demanded that we display approachability and authenticity, all while maintaining a level of vigilance. The mask of unflinching stoicism began to crack, revealing the individuals beneath the uniforms. However, this new vulnerability came with a price - a misstep, an ill-chosen word, could thrust us into the spotlight of criticism and judgment.

This is the story of our evolution from emotional restraint to embracing emotional intelligence, from distant authority figures to approachable allies. Here, we explore the difficulties of being both a guardian of justice and a beacon of empathy, all while proudly carrying the weight of the badge."

Bob M., Lieutenant

A look back

For a moment, let's jump back to May 1854 when, per Wikipedia, the first publicly funded, organized police force with full-time officers was formalized in Boston. The qualifications for being an officer then were that you needed to be firm, strong, and tough. Back then, officer wellness wasn't in anyone's vocabulary, and emotional literacy hadn't even been given a name. It was a different world.

On October 18, 1857, at about 5:15 a.m., Boston first responder Ezekiel W. Hodsdon was patrolling the corner of Havre and Maverick Street in East Boston. Hodsdon attempted to arrest two burglary suspects. A struggle ensued, and one of the suspects was able to get behind Hodsdon and shoot him in the head. Hodsdon died about 10:00 a.m., becoming the first Boston police officer killed in the line of duty.

Officer Hodsdon may have been acting from *honor,* trying to do the right thing. He almost certainly felt *courage* and probably *fear.* The suspects may have acted out of a different *fear, surprise,* or *resentment.* Officer Hodsdon's family and friends experienced emotions. They certainly felt *sorrow, anguish,* and *fury,* but may also have experienced *pride* or *admiration.*

The community collectively experienced emotions. *Anger, fear, frustration,* or *despair* seem likely, but they may also have felt *gratitude* for having had a defender such as Officer Hodsdon. Since we weren't on the scene, we cannot know for sure which emotions were driving each actor's actions, but since emotions generate our behavior, it follows that the emotions of all those involved in this story were key factors in the way it played out.

Emotions have always been a part of policing

Evolution has a purpose, and yet we sometimes can't see it, or we see it but resist. Policing has always been working through periods of change. We all know that first responders complain about two things:

4

The way things are now and change. The change that is currently happening is the recognition of the essential value of emotions and their integration into every aspect of policing.

Whether you are at the beginning or end of your career, emotions are part of your day. Between the time you wake up and your feet hit the floor and the moment you lie down to sleep, you experience thousands of emotions. Most will pass by without your noticing, let alone identifying them, but each one is intimately linked with even your smallest behaviors.

They are your constant companion. They are present in every moment, whether you are awake or asleep. Think about the sweetest dream you've ever had. What made it so sweet? We're betting it was the emotions you felt in your slumber. Recall the worst nightmare you've ever had. What made it so horrible? Emotions and the memory of them you felt on waking.

Every human is an emotional being. Emotions are as much a part of our makeup as breathing, eating, or sleeping. They are not something you get to choose to have or not have. You will have them. Or, perhaps, they will have you. The question each of us has to answer for ourselves is whether we'll waste energy trying to ignore, suppress, or avoid our emotions, or will we be bold enough to embrace and befriend them.

Our evolving perspective

If we take a step back in time, the first IQ (Intelligence Quotient) test was created in 1905. Emotional Quotient (EQ) - was first coined by Reuven Bar-on in 1985. IQ is an *"indicator of intellectual ability and potential."* EQ is commonly understood as *"the ability to interpret and manage emotions effectively."* Compared to the way we assess intellect, we are about 80 years behind in assessing our emotional evaluation and competence.

We all agree EQ is important. However, our current challenge is learning how to turn EQ into a set of habits and a life skill. Doing that requires a commitment to discomfort, self-exploration, and learning. Creating these new invisible habits requires more than a single serving of EQ. Going to the dentist every couple of years to check for cavities would not be described as a rigorous dental hygiene program. Brushing daily, flossing regularly, and bi-annual cleanings are what is needed to maintain healthy gums and teeth. Dental work is expensive. Ignoring it is too.

Why are emotional habits challenging to change?

We cannot see emotions directly. We can see a person's posture and facial expression, or hear the intonation in their speech, but emotions themselves are invisible to the naked eye. That makes them difficult for some people to understand and trust.

Emotions are tools. If I asked you to take the light switch off the wall, you could use a screwdriver, or you could use a hammer, but one is likely to produce damage. When the carpenter does poor work, it is easy for them to blame their tools. But it is not the tools that make us good, but rather how we employ them. Employee Assistance Programs (EAP) can be helpful when you have a traumatic event, but it doesn't matter if the program is not put to use.

First responders get training in ways to defuse situations where emotions run strong, opinions vary, and the stakes are high. Speech, demeanor, posture, and facial expressions can all be taught to better predict someone's behavior. But the source of our behaviors, emotions, are invisible to the naked eye. We talk about the invisible that causes the visible, but we have been slow to link this learning to emotional competence.

Most first responder work comes down to decision-making, problem-solving, and relationship-building. When an officer has been emotionally hijacked, the *visible* is what shows up on a dash cam, body cam, or cell phone. It is the *invisible* that took over. Who is in charge? The thinker or the thought? The emotion or the emoter? Building new, invisible habits may not strike you as easy or familiar. It is, however, essential.

The invisible drives the visible

We aim to help all first responders learn and adopt a structured, clear, operational, and executable process for understanding, exploring, and developing the invisible so that the visible comes into clearer focus. We think of this change as *"you, having success in your evolution."*

We guarantee that this is not "hug a thug" stuff. What is important is that it works. Expanding your emotional toolbox will help you, it will help your family, and it will help the community. Yet, habit is often stronger than reason. Emotional learning can be challenging, unfamiliar, and uncomfortable. Comfort is different from safety; discomfort is necessary, and so is safety. With struggle comes growth.

Policing is always evolving; the question now is, are you willing and able to improve and grow as well?

Gradually, and then Suddenly

We all notice the "suddenly". We talk about the "suddenly". The "suddenly" is what makes the news. But sometimes, what seems sudden has been developing gradually without notice. Divorce does not happen suddenly, it happens gradually. Alcoholism does not happen suddenly, it happens gradually. Suicide does not happen suddenly, it happens gradually. The slippery slope develops gradually into dishonor.

None of us can change "suddenly," but we can influence "gradually." This book is all about the gradual process because that is where change can occur. As you gradually move through your career,

7

there will come a time to "suddenly" step back and retire. When you go to a first responders retirement party, some responders, after 30 + years, are grateful, proud, and excited. They will miss everyone; they have two thumbs up, and their best day is still out ahead of them.

But some first responders, at their retirement party, greet the room with two middle fingers up. They are distant and withdrawn and show disregard for authority. Once they've retired and rolled out the last season of their favorite show, boredom sets in, and it is time to relive all of their many years of work and the decisions they made. It may be difficult, and emotions will flow.

We're not saying one retirement approach is better than the other. What we are saying is that each first responder gets to choose how life will be in their retirement on a daily basis. Your retirement experience will be an extension of how well you navigated your emotions while still on the job.

Your world is gradually evolving. When you realize that it may seem sudden, it may be a surprise to you. The question is how will you choose to adapt to something that has been gradually happening and now is suddenly your reality. Adaptability determines survivability.

Questions to ask yourself

- *How much do you think about the role emotions play in your choices and performance?*
- *What do you observe about the emotions that surface in your agency or with your team?*
- *To what degree are you and those around you being intentional about the emotions you practice and live?*

Practical application

- Set yourself the task of noticing the emotions you experience throughout the day. (In case you have difficulty naming the emotion you are feeling, there is a reference list in the Appendix at the back of the book).

- You may need something to ignite your awareness. How can you randomly bring attention to the emotion you are in? Find a place to keep track of the emotions as you notice them. Bullet points are sufficient. No explanation is required, just noticing and naming.

- Make a running list for a week. Don't judge them; just notice and name them. At the end of the week, take a look back and reflect on:

  - What patterns do you see?
  - How many different emotions did you name?
  - What surprised you?
  - What emotions show up repeatedly?
  - What emotions don't show up that you thought would?
  - What does this tell you about the emotional path you walk during your week?

Chapter 2
Policing and the Power of Perception

*The saying goes that "perception is reality," but it is more accurate to say that "**your** perception is **your** reality."*

Chapter bullets

- Our perception of reality is shaped by our preferences and the things that make us comfortable or not
- I perceive, you perceive, we all perceive…differently
- We're all blind, just to different things

Story

Perceptions

Being an African American police officer can put you amid many perceptions. As a Black officer, you go into the locker room during first watch and hear your brothers in blue share their frustrations about getting an unfair shake in the media. Then, you go home to phone calls of family members voicing their concerns about the loss of those who look like them…and look like you. There were nights I quietly prayed over my children as they slept, unsure of what encounters the next day may bring, and desiring them to return the next day unknown to the media.

A family member called me enraged soon after the news story of Alton Sterling being shot by police was plastered across television. "Man, that's messed up! Another one of us!" I listened to him vent, heard the frustration in his voice, and then asked a pressing question. "If it were me, and I felt a gun in someone's pocket, what would you have wanted me to do?" He paused as he began to give thought. Finally, after quiet deliberation, "I would want you to come home."

I am neither acknowledging wrong nor right in this scenario, but the following:

Seeing life from someone else's eyes is sometimes hard, but if we all did that, more of us would come home. It is not a "Us vs Them" world. It's just "us," human beings needing to see one another and value what we see.

Gerald H., Assistant to the City Manager

How we see dictates everything

I, Marcel, remember a good friend who had just learned to drive, and her father stressed that if she ever felt she was in danger or needed help, to seek the help of a first responder. Her father pointed out where the police stations were in her neighborhood, around her school, and near her grandmother's house. There, she would find a person who was sworn to protect and serve her.

I have since heard others describe learning the opposite attitude toward police and police stations. This group grew up hearing that they should avoid the police and locations where police were likely to be. Some describe avoiding the vicinity or roads where there were police stations or learning never to make eye contact with a patrol officer.

Perceptions about you, a first responder, are formed early. "To protect and serve?" "To hassle and harm?" A person you seek out when you're in trouble? A person you intentionally avoid making sure your paths never cross?

These simple descriptions of behavior point to the range of perceptions of first responders. Our perceptions depend on our race, age, gender, community we grew up in, ethnic background, prior experience, and almost certainly our history of interactions or lack of interactions with police. They also depend on what our family and friends say and what we hear on social media, TV, radio, and from other sources of information.

Those who rely solely on national news for their information would be hard-pressed to have a positive perception of first responders. They are exposed every day to images of police shooting and killing Black men, Hispanic men, and other events that appear to show that police are not focused on apprehending criminals but are regularly involved in unjustified use of force.

Ironically, when these items make the news, it is because your profession is still a noble one. It shows that there is still trust in first responders. When first responders don't do their best work, it is reported. You can take comfort in the fact that it is still so uncommon that it is newsworthy. When police misconduct is no longer newsworthy, we will know that the profession has failed its citizens.

What is perception?

It is the way we see and understand reality. It is not reality. It looks like reality to us, and we often confuse our perception with what is real and true, but they are different things. We sometimes refer to perception as our mindset, beliefs, understanding, or perspective. They are all ways of seeing what is, but only from one angle, ours.

Besides an accurate perception, we are also capable of having an inaccurate perception, an incomplete perception, and/or a missing perception. Interestingly, we often cannot see we have a misperception until someone points it out to us. What we see, hear, and feel about a topic is all we know about it.

Unconsciously, we tend to believe those things we think are best or true or preferable. Because we tend to believe our perspective is the truth, we sometimes judge others wrong when they believe differently. We do not see ourselves as we really are. We do not see the world as it really is. When we increase our self-awareness and our others-awareness it enables us to show up more intentionally to allow for each person's lived truth and can let it to exist alongside ours.

Imagine you are walking down the street. You notice someone you recognize walking toward you. As they pass, you say "hello," but they walk by without returning your greeting or acknowledging you. What just happened? Well, there are the observable facts, and there is your perception. Your perception could be that the person ignored you, they don't like you, they're angry with you, they're a jerk, they didn't hear you, they were preoccupied because someone they care about is in trouble, and on and on.

When we go through life without correcting our inaccurate perceptions, they can become chronic. Chronic diseases are those that never go away. As a result, others feel the dis-ease of our blind spots and the blind behaviors they cause. Said differently, rude people are rude because somewhere in their lives, they were rewarded for their rude behaviors and are blind to the impact it has on others. One small shift in perception can achieve a big shift in behavior and performance.

Blind Spots Cause Blind Behaviors

You might say that we're all blind, just in different ways. We all have blind spots in our knowledge and opinions. The bad news is that blind spots can keep us from recognizing the behaviors they generate, which gives us false confidence in our perspective. Blindness even prevents us from reflecting on or reconsidering our actions. The good news is that we can look for our blind spots and begin to see what was previously invisible.

Types of blindness

"When you are dead, you do not know you are dead, and all the pain is felt by others."

Author unknown

The brain is a marvelous thing but not infallible. Here are four ways our brains can blind us:

- **Self-Justification:** As we see the situation unfolding, our brain starts to inform us how it believes we need to behave to survive. This allows us to justify what are sometimes foolish beliefs, bad decisions, and hurtful acts. Self-initiated inactivity, entitlement, and "pencil whipping" are a few examples that officers sometimes self-justify.

- **Moral Intuition:** Experiences call forth our moral beliefs, which are durable insofar as they are tightly held and resist counterevidence. Sometimes, strong data can influence us to change our moral beliefs, but most of the time, it does not. Some individuals see alcoholism as a willpower issue and not a disease. After providing the individual with a significant amount of information that alcoholism is indeed a disease, they say something like, "I don't know...it just doesn't feel right". Self-justification and moral intuition make us righteously certain that those who see things differently than us are wrong.

- **Blind Spot Bias:** People who believe they don't suffer from blind spots are more likely to ignore the advice of other people and are less likely to benefit from learning and development geared to reduce their commission of other biases. Thinking you do not snore as you listen to a recording of yourself snoring loudly is a blind spot.

14

- **Private Logic:** People do what they do because, to them, it makes sense. Think of private logic as an invisible backpack. A backpack full of rationales for why we do what we do. Why do people leave their vehicles unlocked? Why do people leave their property unattended in public areas? If you were to ask them, they would have a reason that makes sense to them.

Case in point: Someone changes lanes on the freeway and you think of it as cutting you off. Why did they do that? Because it made sense to them. Why did you label it "cutting me off?" Because that is what made sense to you. That is what most of us experience when we judge other people's behaviors. What if we perceived them as unaware? They had no idea they cut you off in traffic. What if this is a kind, considerate person on their way to church? Let's stop assigning motives to others and seek to understand what moves them to do what they do.

Just like a car has mirrors to help you see what is blocked from your direct view, each of us needs help to see our cognitive blind spots. One significant tool that can help us is awareness: sensing that something is occurring in or around us even if we can't see it.

Self-awareness allows us to reflect on what we are thinking, feeling, or experiencing and challenges us to reflect on what we believe to be true. Asking others for their perspective helps us see what is hidden from our view of ourselves. Others-awareness reveals what others are feeling, may need, and the impact we are having on them.

Without awareness, we tend to live life mechanically, mostly attending to our immediate desires or needs. Awareness is key to understanding ourselves and others, and in building relationships. Every first responder lives in a vast network of relationships, which means that lack of awareness will impede every part of their self-understanding and work.

How we see ourselves

You and I do not see reality the same. There is one, but we only see part of it. That is what often generates a gap or misunderstanding. You may believe you have the most important message in the world, but the person on the receiving end will always understand it through the prism of his or her own preconceptions, prejudices, pre-existing beliefs, and emotions. Humans have a relationship with everything they encounter. You relate to and have preferences and opinions about the weather, your relatives, money, work, baseball, sushi…everything that exists. You also have a relationship with yourself.

How do you picture yourself, think about yourself, value yourself, and, therefore, treat yourself? The simplest way to answer this question is to listen to your thoughts about yourself. If you regularly think, "I'm okay" or "I'm as valuable as every other person," you have a relationship that is based on dignity and self-respect. If you judge and criticize yourself or berate yourself for making mistakes, you relate to yourself from impatience, contempt, or dislike. If you focus mostly on how attractive you are to others, you relate to yourself through the emotions of vanity or conceit. How you think about yourself and the emotions associated with those thoughts reflect your self-perception.

When first responders have an account on LinkedIn, some use a picture that has them in uniform, some are pictured with their family, some are smiling, some are not, and others use a picture of them in sunglasses, gloves, a smedium shirt sitting in or leaning up against their vehicle. The image an officer selects is a window into their self-perception.

How you see yourself makes a difference in your actions. If you have a low opinion of yourself, you may put your effort into trying to show others how important you are in either constructive or not-so-constructive ways. If you see yourself as confident and capable, you will simply get on with it. Emotions have everything to do with how you see yourself. One reason to expand your emotional understanding is to have the humility to take an honest look at yourself. Humility is the only ticket available to be at peace with ourselves. When you decrease ego, increase self-awareness, and your ability to share yourself, it helps you unlock creativity, connection, and performance.

To what degree do I know and accept all of me?

There are certain things that make you feel good about yourself, but if you do not accept your character defects, you will not admit your character defects. If you do not own your insecurities, they will own you. If you do not accept that maybe you are too direct when speaking with others, you will never acknowledge it. Intent and tone is the difference between being assertive and being rude. If you do not accept that you are an alcoholic, you will not admit that you are an alcoholic. Own where you are. Pretending to be someone or something you are not does not work. Become aware. Accept. Admit. Evolve.

There is an adage that says, "Change takes time." It is more accurate to say that change takes one moment, the moment you accept that what you are doing is no longer working. Said differently, you can't change what you tolerate. Once you are done tolerating something, you can declare that it is time to do it differently.

17

An unaware person is dangerous.

Just like on the street, if you are situationally unaware, you put others in danger. The unaware person is just that, unaware. They do not know the blind spots which are causing their blind behaviors. They do not know how they make decisions, solve problems, and build relationships. You do not know you have a misperception until someone tells you. A friend of ours suggests that if one person tells you that you have a tail, you can probably ignore them, but if two people tell you, you should probably check.

It is our inner game that creates our outer game. That is why an officer can be fully armed and get emotionally hijacked. What we are suggesting is that we can prepare ourselves to avoid becoming emotionally disarmed.

How one sees dictates everything. The only way we succeed in our evolution is by seeing things differently, thus changing the story we tell ourselves. Self-awareness is one of the most important and often missing "skills" of people in positions of authority, which is you.

Extraordinary leaders possess and practice extraordinary self-awareness. Self-awareness allows you to also have emotional hygiene, which is the practice of taking care of your emotions with the same diligence as you do (or should) take care of your body.

You can't out-recruit a retention problem. Nothing happens until it happens to you

When I (Marcel) was 19, I had a chance to help a colleague feel heard and comforted, but I ended up doing the opposite. I was in the U.S. Army stationed in Schofield Barracks, Hawaii. It was in the Army that I had an experience that revealed my blindness and changed my understanding of myself forever.

18

One of my Ranger buddies had lost his father. As he was sharing with me, I replied, "I understand." He asked me if I had lost my father as well, and I replied, "No, my father is still alive." He looked at me and shook his head. My statement was meaningless because I didn't yet know how to accurately empathize.

Below are a few examples that help illustrate this concept:

- Most parents have received unsolicited advice from a non-parent. It may have been shared with the best intentions, but it is clear that it comes from a person who has not lived parenthood.

- If you have never loved a dog with all of your heart, waited tables, been overweight, served in the military, taught Sunday school, been in the minority, or been an officer who has been pulled over or accused of a crime, please do not think that "you know what it is like" because you don't.

- If you have never lost a child or had a parent with Parkinson's or dementia, the best you can do is be sympathetic, not empathetic. Sympathy means "to feel for," and empathy means "to feel with."

If someone cares enough to share that they believe you are blind in some way, receive it as a gift.

Ego can be thought of as our perception of self. Ego reveals what we believe about ourselves. We may believe we are strong or weak, smart or stupid, capable or incapable. How you perceive yourself influences everything you think and do.

We see two key formulas related to self-perception:

1. **Self-awareness + Others Awareness = Intentionality**.

19

- Self-awareness = Intellectual Humility

- Others-awareness = Cultural Humility

- Intentionality = How am I showing up, and am I helping others feel safe and respected?

When we maintain awareness of ourselves and others simultaneously, we can balance self-interest with care. That is a balance we all need.

2. **Self-awareness > Ego**. Believing that our view of the world is correct is comforting, but self-awareness is more powerful. Self-awareness is the mega skill of the 21st century. One of the most effective ways to rein in ego is by strengthening self-awareness. High ego and high self-awareness rarely run together.

What about ego?

What we refer to as ego, or 'sense of self,' has its own set of biases.

- Big or exaggerated egos are often the result of a bias called *illusory superiority*. That is the tendency to overestimate one's desirable qualities and underestimate one's undesirable qualities. There is also the *moral credential effect*, which occurs when we do something good and that leads us to believe we are entitled to do less good, or even harmful, in the future.

- A small or underdeveloped ego can show up as timidity, lack of assertiveness, or self-doubt. The most common bias associated with a low sense of self is *imposter syndrome,* or the belief that you are pretending to be more competent than you are and will eventually be found out.

Awareness is the key, and action opens the door.

The pendulum of policing has a tendency to swing back and forth, reflecting the ever-evolving nature of law enforcement practices and public sentiment. At times, there may be a shift towards stricter law enforcement approaches, emphasizing crime control and proactive measures. The events surrounding the killing of Michael Brown in 2014 raised many questions and sparked a nationwide debate about policing in the United States. The incident in Ferguson, Missouri, and the subsequent protests highlighted the complexities that law enforcement officers face in their work, as well as the underlying issues of systemic bias that can affect police-community relations.

Michael Brown's death served as a catalyst for law enforcement agencies, communities, policymakers, and activists to come together to critically examine the role of policing in our society. While the incident was a focal point for the Black Lives Matter movement, it also prompted law enforcement professionals to engage in thoughtful dialogue about how to build trust, increase transparency, and promote accountability within their ranks.

Since then, the national conversation around policing has continued to evolve, emphasizing the importance of community engagement and exploring alternative approaches to traditional law enforcement that prioritize safety and mutual respect. This swing of the pendulum reflects the ongoing efforts to strike a delicate balance between effective crime prevention and the fair, equitable treatment of all individuals within the communities being served. The challenge being faced is for first responders to adapt appropriately.

Moreover, the media has the power to influence the narrative surrounding police-community relations, shaping the public's understanding of complex issues. Coverage that emphasizes conflict, division, or polarizing perspectives can fuel a sense of mistrust between law enforcement and the communities they serve. Conversely, media outlets that prioritize balanced reporting, foster dialogue, and highlight community engagement efforts can help build understanding and bridge the gap between the first responder and the public.

As consumers of news, it is important for the public to critically evaluate media narratives, seek diverse perspectives, and be mindful of potential biases. By being informed and engaged, individuals can contribute to a more nuanced understanding of law enforcement issues and support efforts to improve police-community relations. Ultimately, the media has a responsibility to uphold journalistic integrity, present a balanced view of policing, and foster an informed public discourse that promotes transparency, accountability, and the pursuit of justice. Whether they take that responsibility seriously is another matter.

How we see others

Our perception of others is generally based on what we've learned from those around us, what we've learned from personal experiences, and our biases.

A few of the biases that shape our perception of others are:

- **Unconscious bias:** The underlying attitudes and stereotypes that we unconsciously attribute to another person or group of people that affect how we understand and engage with them. Malcolm Gladwell writes in his book "Blink" that snap judgments are, first of all, enormously quick. They rely on the thinnest slices of experience and are unconscious. Even when we don't pre-judge, research at Princeton showed it can take as little as 1/10th of a second to form our opinion of another person.

- **Stereotyping:** Expecting a member of a group to have certain characteristics without any information about that individual.

- **Confirmation bias**: The tendency to search for, interpret, favor, and recall information in a way that confirms or supports one's prior beliefs or values.

- **Compassion fade:** The tendency to behave more compassionately towards a small number of identifiable victims than to a large number of anonymous ones.

Your unconscious biases will show up as you read through the following list. They won't necessarily be negative. You may find yourself nodding in approval for some of them.

- Uvalde
- Covid 19
- Hoodies
- Patrol Ball Caps
- Cite and release
- Beards & tattoos
- No pursuit policy
- Unhoused people
- Take-home vehicles
- Kneeling at a protest
- Marijuana decriminalization
- Incomplete report from hysterical caller
- University, municipality, and ISD officers
- Someone who was promoted too quickly
- Officer studying for promotion while on duty
- A co-worker who talks only about retirement
- Attending the FBINA or PERF leadership program
- An officer taking an entire month off to study for the promotion test

What did you find yourself thinking or feeling as you read?

Just as we have a habitual way of relating to ourselves, we have a typical way of relating to others. We can feel appreciation, respect, intrigue, contempt, disdain, or revulsion. Just as being aware of our ego matters because it determines what we do or don't do, other perception does as well. We sometimes treat people based not on the current interaction, but based on our perception of who they are and, therefore what they deserve. The point of consideration is whether we treat people based on who they are or based on our perception of who we think they should be.

How others see us

In today's interconnected world, the media plays a significant role in shaping public perception, and this holds true as well for the portrayal of law enforcement agencies. The media acts as a powerful intermediary, influencing how the public perceives the police and 911 through its coverage, narratives, and presentation of events. National events influence local perceptions. The way incidents involving the police/911 telecommunicators are reported can either reinforce or challenge existing biases, and it is crucial to recognize the impact that media coverage has on shaping public opinion in only a few seconds.

The media's portrayal of the police can contribute to the formation of stereotypes and biases, which can be influenced by factors such as the framing of stories, sensationalism, and selective coverage. Instances of police misconduct, 911 hanging up on callers, or controversial encounters are often given more prominence, leading to a perception that such incidents are more prevalent than they may actually be.

This selective focus can create a skewed image of law enforcement, overshadowing the vast majority of positive interactions and acts of service performed by officers on a daily basis. Just as we have perceptions and biases about others, they have them about us. Unconscious bias (stereotyping), bias blind spot (believing we're less biased than others), naïve realism (the belief that what we see is reality), and confirmation bias (looking for evidence to support what we already believe) are certainly present in the way certain others see us.

Regarding your social media consumption, we suggest that you find a middle ground. Rolling your social media window all the way down can be overwhelming, while keeping it fully up can leave you in the dark. Instead, we suggest keeping your window cracked, allowing you to filter and respond to social media content in a thoughtful and appropriate manner. This approach ensures that you engage with social media responsibly, avoiding emotional overload and enabling effective communication.

How others see themselves

The biases we've discussed are present in how others see themselves as well. When they lack awareness of those biases and the blindness they create others will believe what they are seeing because it makes sense to them.

It is food for thought that we tend to judge others by their behaviors, but judge ourselves by our intentions.

At this point, you may be asking yourself why we have biases if they distort our perception. Wouldn't it be better to just see things as they are? It turns out that, according to Smithsonian Magazine, "Bias is how our minds streamline thinking so we can quickly make sense of the world. Our brains are biologically designed to perform these quick judgments unconsciously. In early prehistory, this unconscious, streamlined thinking was a form of protection against threats from the natural world.".

In other words, bias is a survival mechanism. It is part of our makeup as humans. It is unavoidable but part of the time is unhelpful. At times we may feel it is not fair to be assessed or judged without being known, but it happens and will continue to happen.

Knowing that there are limits to our perception, we have the responsibility to learn all we can about how they develop and influence us. If we read and hear mostly positive news about policing, our perception will likely remain positive. If we read and hear mostly negative news about policing, our perception will probably lean toward the negative. For this reason, police departments strive to establish and maintain a positive image in the eyes of the community, focused on their role as protectors and servants of the public.

Finally

What this all boils down to is that every human has biases and pre-judges situations and others. That is not going to change. That gives us two options: Continue as we are ignoring the possibility of expanding our awareness or embrace their permanency and learn how to notice, name, and navigate them. We can choose to prepare ourselves for the moment our misperceptions show up and when they show up in others.

Ignorance and misunderstanding are what cause the dis-ease of perception. We can do better.

Questions to ask yourself

- What assumptions or biases might you be holding that could hinder your understanding or perspective?
- What feedback or criticism do you tend to dismiss or become defensive about?
- Are there problematic patterns in your relationships or interactions that seem to repeat?
- Do you tend to dismiss or ignore information that contradicts your existing beliefs or opinions?
- What do you think people see when they see you coming?

Practical application

Ask several people you trust some of the following questions:

- Where do they notice that you may be perceiving a situation or person incorrectly?
- What do they see that makes them believe that?
- Are there any patterns or behaviors in your relationships or interactions that seem to lead to negative outcomes in their opinion?
- What consequences do they think that is producing in your life?
- What consequences do they see that is creating for the situation or in the life of the other person?

Chapter 3
Yes, and...

"I did then what I knew how to do. Now that I know better, I do better."

- Maya Angelou

Chapter bullets:

- What is power?
- Who holds it?
- How power and emotions are interconnected

Story

Present and Authentic

Throughout my twenty-seven years of service, I have had the opportunity to witness many friends and colleagues retire. I have had numerous discussions with others about their retirements. Without fail, during these discussions or their retirement ceremonies, they talked about their wish to spend more time with their families and loved ones. They talked about the sacrifices of time and the moments they missed with their families throughout their careers.

This book, this chapter, and these authors are teaching that each moment, each day, with each emotion we encounter, we can choose how we respond. We are responsible for our own decisions and our happiness. That is a powerful and potentially life-changing lesson; all we must do is be willing to be uncomfortable and learn.

We, as law enforcement, must learn from our brothers and sisters in the military and fire departments. They train daily, weekly, and

28

monthly to protect freedom and fight fires. Law Enforcement trains less frequently, sometimes once a month or once a year. We tell ourselves that the military and fire departments are not always fighting wars or fires and they have time to train. We must change our way of thinking and make time daily, weekly, and monthly to train on force continuum and other essential police functions. This book is advocating that we train our emotional intelligence the same way. Daily, every moment and every reaction we have to our emotions is our decision, our choice.

This means we alone are responsible for our own happiness. We have the decision to be present every moment with our family and friends. We get to determine our emotions every shift and every call for service. We can choose to build authentic relationships with the people in our lives. We can choose to retire with no regrets and no lost time.

Yes, it will take daily practice and training, but what a powerful tool to know that you alone control your happiness. Don't give that power away; train your mind and own your emotions.

Stay vigilant!

Marc S., Captain

What this book is not about

Previously, we stated what this book is about. Now, let us state what it is not about:
- It is not about finding or laying blame
- It is not to talk about having done things wrong
- It is not written to provoke shame or regret

All of us are where we are because we made choices with the knowledge and skills available to us. The current situation in policing is the result of millions of choices made over many decades. No one laid out a plan for understaffing, societal division and unrest, or tension levels that can damage an officer's well-being. Most of what we see around us was not created intentionally. We worked with the knowledge and tools available, and like in most other fields, the tools we have today reveal the limitations of the tools we had yesterday.

Reports of unwarranted exertion of power, deliberate and harmful actions, and discourteous conduct toward ordinary citizens will only diminish when such incidents cease to occur. Harmful actions must become as infrequent as aviation accidents in order to shift the prevailing perspective of law enforcement towards the mission every chief characterizes as the core purpose of their department and every officer in their ranks. The servant leader is a servant first. If you are a shepherd, you should smell like sheep.

What the authors want to suggest is that in spite of our best efforts, we can now see that we've missed some fundamentals, and those have blocked improvement and progress. Part of the reason we've missed them is that they didn't exist and are ideas and perspectives only now emerging. The other reason is that our perspective at the time didn't allow us to see their potential value.

In the jigsaw puzzle we're all trying to solve, the authors see two pieces missing:

- The first is understanding and accepting the relative power of organizations vs individuals to create change

- The second is the pivotal role emotions play in the process of improvement

Power balance

Let's begin with the question of power. How many times have you heard that "knowledge is power?" There could be nothing more untrue. Knowledge, both intellectual and emotional, applied is power.

You could be the smartest person on the planet and never share what you know. You would have no power. A big reason why many people see power as negative is because it has been applied to them unfairly at some point in their life.

Power is neutral. Power is a tool similar to a handgun, not inherently good or bad. Power can be applied, balanced, and shared. Power is defined by the Oxford Dictionary as *"the capacity or ability to direct or influence the behavior of others or the course of events."*

We (Dan and Marcel) notice that we sometimes attribute more power (and thus, responsibility) to organizations than is warranted, and we sometimes do not attribute as much power (and thus, responsibility) to individuals as is needed.

Let's take a closer look. In terms of your development as a professional, what percentage is the responsibility of the agency, and what is the responsibility of the officers? What does any organization have the power to "direct or influence?" Standards, resources, policy, infrastructure, protocols, proper training, operational values, and other institutional elements are all examples. What does an agency not have the power to do? An agency cannot make its employees believe or behave in specific ways, force an individual to feel a certain emotion, or care about what the agency is committed to.

Mary Wollstonecraft, the famous British writer, wrote that "A man convinced against his will is of the same opinion still." **Procedures reflect desired regulation but are powerless to**

generate self-regulation in individuals. Thus, the ability to self-regulate emotions by each and every first responder is crucial. That is where the power is.

When other alcoholics ask me, Marcel, to be their sponsor, I let them know upfront that the most I can give to their sobriety is 49%. I cannot want them to be more sober than they want to be. In order for this relationship to work, I'll give my 49%, but they have to give 51%.

Similarly, no agency can have more than a 49% say in how its employees behave. It does not matter how attentive or well-intentioned the agency is; that is all the power it can ever have.

Police leaders would often like it to be different. They expect to have control because how else can they lead? They are expected to influence the agency they lead by the community, the press, and other observers. They make promises based on the premise that they can control employee behaviors and outcomes. Life, for them, would be easier if they had full control. It is tough for them to admit they don't.

So, if a police department only holds 49% of the cards, who holds the other 51%? The individuals. It is their behavior that is seen. It is they who generate the perceptions others have and give the agency its character. This means that if true change is to occur, it needs to focus not just on the agency, but on every individual. The level at which employees are treated well inside the agency is directly correlated to how well they treat citizens on the street, and it is a leader's job to set the environment, but they are not responsible for the results. Every individual is.

Emotions

Agencies themselves do not feel emotions. It is inaccurate to say that an agency cares, feels compassion, or has desires because, while humans make up a police department, it cannot sense; only humans can. The leaders, present and past, may have led from those emotions, but when the leader changes sometimes the emotional climate changes.

Yet, every team member's emotions play a part in generating the emotional climate of the agency. Specific emotions are not inherent in the agency itself but are the property of the people. When a new chief takes charge, they cannot single-handedly shift the emotions of the agency. Everyone holds a piece of the emotional puzzle.

Every individual in the agency experiences emotions. Some may try to avoid or deny them, but emotions are part of our human makeup and not something we get to choose. If you combine emotions' inevitability with what we said previously, that the agency cannot dictate the emotions of the individual, and add the fact that the majority of a first responder's day and work is done alone, you begin to see the missing piece.

Departments have done and continue to do an enormous amount of training, instruction, and learning with their staff, yet have not addressed the importance of each person's emotions. Once the training and learning concludes, the factor that determines how a first responder will behave is his or her emotional competence.

Here's a model that shows why:

Foundational Model

Competence:
The sum of all the training experience, practice, and learning that you've undergone

Emotion:
The filter that regulates the degree to which your competence is reflected in your actions

Action:
What you do when the moment arrive

No matter how deep or wide training your competence is in a traditional sense, it is incomplete without the emotional component. Emotions are what activate 'knowing how.'

Some emotions support intervention, and others act as barriers.

Emotions and Intervention

Supportive emotions	Barrier emotions
• Dignity	• Fear
• Humility	• Shame
• Honesty	• Embarrassment
• Honor	• Guilt
• Compassion	• Resentment
• Love	• Denial
• Trust	• Resignation
• Faith	• Anger

The emotion or emotions a first responder experiences as the situation unfolds are co-created with their thoughts or beliefs. And a first responder's thoughts can be about many things.

If they are thinking about...

- the citizen, they might feel *fear, compassion, or honor.*
- their supervisor, they might feel *loyalty, dread, or desire* to please.
- their safety, their emotions might be *anxiety, anger, or self-respect.*
- their colleagues, their emotions might include *disbelief, trust, or hope.*
- the community, their emotions might be *service, disappointment, or empathy.*
- the telecommunicator, their emotions might be *obligation, urgency, or uncertainty.*

You might imagine we're only talking above about an arrest scenario, but the model applies equally to a telecommunicator, a detention staff, or one who is resisting self-reporting for exhaustion or concerns about their mental well-being. It applies as well to peer reporting.

For self-reporting and peer reporting, the table of emotions looks slightly different than for duty to intervene, but the principle remains the same.

Supportive emotions	Barrier emotions
Dignity	Shame
Humility	Embarrassment
Honesty	Guilt
Gratitude	Fear
Intolerance	Loyalty
Self-compassion	Resentment
Love	Denial
Self-trust	Naivete
Faith	Resignation
Self-respect	Resentment
Acceptance	Ambivalence

No matter what policies are in place, they will only be implemented if the emotions individuals can access enables that to happen. Otherwise, a policy will just remain a great idea. In weak cultures, people find safety in rules. That is how we get bureaucrats. In strong cultures, people find safety in relationships. Rules – Relationships = Rebellion.

$$1 + 1 = 3$$

So, does all of this mean that police departments can do less and expect their officers to do more? Absolutely not! What it means is that a department that is striving with all its might, wisdom, and resources can only contribute 49% to the effort. And that is their responsibility. Every officer, if aware, trained, and emotionally aligned, can contribute 51%. And that is their responsibility.

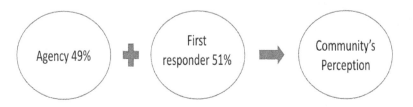

When that happens, the community gets 100%. However, life, being imperfect as it is, we all know that is naive to imagine. With that being said, we can understand that the closer we get to the maximum we can contribute, the better off we all will be.

Organizations generate a unique quality called context. 'Context' is what gives meaning to 'text.' If I hand you a $10 bill, it means nothing without context. Did you drop it, and I'm returning it to you, or am I offering to purchase your car? The word strike, without context, can mean a mass work stoppage or it can be swinging at a pitched ball and missing or knocking down all 10 pins on a bowling lane or physically hitting someone.

The essential role the agency can play in aligning the two missing puzzle pieces is:

- Declare its mission, vision, values, principles, and desires for what it wants to become.
- Create and insist on a safe and respectful space for all employees to explore and learn about emotions and the power emotions generate.

Without those contextual pieces, officers will often experience what has been recently labeled psychological homelessness, "a lack of a sense of worth, purpose and belonging in an individual. It is an utter lack of a loving, caring and protective environment where they feel happy and content with their relationships".

The essential things every individual can do are:

- Reframe their understanding of emotions as a competency and skill
- Commit to taking responsibility for building their emotional literacy, fluency, and mastery

"Historically, there is a widely held belief within the fields where I worked that if you're tough enough and cool enough and committed to your cause enough, you'll keep on keeping on, you'll suck it up. Self-care is something for the weaker set." from "Trauma Stewardship" by Laura van Dernoot Lipsky with Connie Burk.

What humans are beginning to realize is that for all its magnificence and power, reason is not the only basis of knowledge; we've overlooked a life-enhancing tool called emotions.

Questions to ask yourself

- What is an emotion you could dial back to better meet people where they need to be met? (For reference, we've provided a list of emotions in the Appendix)
- What is an emotion that, if you dialed up, could help you relationally, positionally, personally, or financially?
- What would life be like if you were able to let go of the thoughts in your head that produce emotions that are no longer serving you?
- What emotions does your mind need to consent to your heart having?
- Would your agency put more effort into this area of learning if it was understood that in the moment of action, more than half of the choice rests on the first responder's emotions?
- What importance should you place on your emotional fitness, knowing that 51% of the responsibility depends on your preparation?

Practical application

- Make a short list of the emotions you think are needed for sworn and professional staff to see each other as respected and valued.
- Investigate the available resources and support systems for officers' emotional well-being in your agency. How can you promote their utilization?
- Look for an opportunity to encourage others to provide emotional support to a colleague.

Chapter 4
"But wait! What are Emotions?"

"Care for your psyche...know thyself, for once we know ourselves, we may learn how to care for ourselves."

- Socrates

Chapter bullets

- Emotions are not what you thought they were
- Emotions are logical
- Emotions are not a weakness, they are a core competency and life skill

Story

Hope

It fuels all things. It is an emotion; it is not a weakness. To prove this point, in 1957, Dr. Curt Richter, an American psycho-biologist, conducted an experiment with rats to determine their survivability. Beginning with domesticated rats, Dr. Richter put 12 rats into water jars separately to determine how long they would swim, and thus survive. Nine of the 12 lasted as long as 60 hours. Believing that wild rats would do even better given their mandate to survive, he exposed them to the same conditions. Wild rats are renowned for their swimming ability, but to Dr. Richter's surprise, these rats died within minutes of entering the water. Why? The answer: Hope.

Dr. Richter discovered that because of support mechanisms associated with being a domesticated rat, there was a direct correlation between giving up and their belief that rescue may be at hand. To prove this point, he conducted the experiment with an additional variable. After placing wild rats into the water, but before they died, he would pull them from the water and allow them to recover. They would then be immersed again, and this was repeated several times. The result: even the wild rats lasted 60 hours before finally succumbing to exhaustion and drowning. Said differently, these rats were given hope that they would be rescued, so they never gave up. Only sheer exhaustion killed them, but it took days for that to happen. Hope, it seems, was the difference-maker. They went from minutes of survival to days, all because they knew there was a chance they would survive.

Dr. Richter wrote, "After elimination of hopelessness, the rats do not die." The same is true for humans, and this story proves the value and power of emotions. There are ample medical studies documenting patients who die suddenly with non-fatal injuries, precisely because they have no hope or desire.

We all need to keep swimming! We all need to recognize the value of hope. Hope is an emotion; it is also a life source.

Stan S., Chief of Police

(On the Phenomenon of Sudden Death in Animals and Man, Richter C., 1957)

It may sound harsh, but emotions don't care what you think about them. They don't care if you are comfortable or uncomfortable, whether you like them or not. They show up to do a job, to take care of you in some way. If you choose to deny or ignore them, that will have consequences for you, not for them.

Notice which emotions came up as you read this story. Manuscript reviewers mentioned to us that they felt revulsion, disgust, pity, surprise, incredulity, anger, hope, sadness, and several others. You may have experienced one or more of them as well. Whichever it was for you, don't judge it right or wrong or try to chase it away. Simply observe. Notice. What physical feelings were stirred? What were your thoughts? Can you name your emotion or emotions? Why do you think that emotion showed up for you, but different emotions were sparked for others? What is the purpose of the emotion you experienced? These are the questions that will be explored in the following chapters.

A fundamental practice we are going to invite you to repeatedly is to **notice, name, and navigate** your emotions. These three steps form the basis of emotional learning and eventual mastery. You will see them again.

Myths and misconceptions about emotions

Everything is not necessarily as you learned it was. "Einstein failed math," ... "a penny dropped from the top of the Empire State Building could kill someone," ... "touching a toad will give you warts," ..." lightning never strikes the same place twice". All untrue.

Our understanding of emotions is loaded with myths and misconceptions. You can debunk many based on your experiences:

- **"Emotions are positive or negative"**: *Fear* keeps us safe. *Fear* keeps us from doing things we want. So, is *fear* positive or negative? Neither. As with all emotions, it is either serving us or not, depending on the situation.
- **"You can avoid your emotions"**: In your sleep, you experience emotions. Sweet dreams are the result of pleasant emotions; nightmares are populated by unpleasant emotions. You experience emotions while asleep, awake, and in every other moment of your life.
- **"You can't learn emotionally"**: If that were true, you'd have the same emotional capacity and range as a newborn. Clearly, that is not the case. People say,

"That's just the way I am". Maybe, or maybe, it is the way they have learned to be.

- **"Emotions get in the way of clear thinking"**: If you think good things are likely to happen, you experience *optimism*. If you think bad things are likely to happen, you experience *pessimism*. Emotions and thinking are inseparable. Try choosing the emotion that will help you think the way you want to think.

- **"You can't trust emotions"**: *Curiosity* prompts you to find out more, *loyalty* to defend those you care about, *joy* to celebrate, and *anger* lets you know that you are encountering injustice. We can learn to trust that emotions have a message and purpose.

- **"You need to control your emotions"**: I can't, you can't, no one we have ever met can. What does that suggest? Maybe control isn't the best way to relate to our emotions. Perhaps considering that our emotions are a tool to help us navigate life would be more effective.

- **"Emotions should be left at the door"**: There is no organization on earth that does not want its employees to feel *ambition, passion, curiosity, loyalty, inspiration, or enthusiasm*, yet those are some of the emotions that would be excluded from the workplace if we followed this suggestion.

Exercise:

Think back to all the messages you remember receiving about emotions while growing up. Make a list of them. They may be things you were taught, things you overheard others say, or things you made up in an attempt to understand the mysterious force we call emotions.

Some of the misconceptions that we regularly hear from clients, no matter where they grew up, their level of education, or the work they do today, are that:

- *I was told to hide my emotions*
- *Emotions are only about hugging and crying*
- *Showing emotions is unmanly*
- *Expressing emotions is inappropriate*
- *They're a waste of time*
- *Emotions make you look weak*
- *Emotions can't be trusted*
- *They will steer you wrong*

Take a look at your list and ask yourself if all the things on your list are verifiable. Are they true, or are they just what you learned?

Reframing emotions

One of our most profound human desires is to understand. We search for ways to understand how and why things happen. Sometimes, that understanding helps keep us safe and other times, it allows us to do things we could not previously do. When our current understanding seems inadequate we have a clever methodology we employ that allows us to understand better. We develop a new theory. The theory is a new interpretation that attempts to make our experiences more understandable or useful.

For a long time, we've thought that emotions were about hugging, kissing, and crying, and that they were defined, in part, by the misconceptions listed above. That is the old interpretation of emotions we've lived by. In the evolution of understanding what it means to be human, it is time for a reframe.

If we were to start from a clean sheet of paper and articulate what emotions are, it would look something like this:

Emotions are:

- **"The energy that moves us":** A translation from the original Latin would be "that that sets in motion." The Romans cleverly avoided having to articulate what "that" was, but were clear in their belief that emotions are a force that moves us.

- **Unavoidable:** Emotions are non-discretionary; that is, we don't get to decide whether we'll have emotions. They are a biological process that is part of our makeup. Emotions work in a similar way to sleep. We get to decide where we sleep, when we sleep, how we sleep, and who we sleep with, but we don't get to decide **if** we'll sleep. Sleep cannot be avoided and is a natural part of being human. Emotions are similar. We have the latitude to decide how we understand and relate to emotions, whether we fight or embrace them, whether we listen to or ignore them, and whether we react or respond, **but** we do not get to decide **if** we'll have emotions. We are emotional beings.

- **A domain of knowledge:** We know things intellectually, and we know things emotionally. Emotions tell us things that reason cannot. We often feel things before we think them. Emotions are constantly giving us information about what is happening around us and within us.

- **Neutral:** Every emotion has the potential to either serve us or to be a barrier. Even ambition, which is revered as positive in many organizations, can be a barrier when it interferes with service, honesty, honor, loyalty, or our ability to rest and restore ourselves. This concept is often difficult for us to embrace and remember because we have a deeply ingrained habit of thinking about emotions as positive or negative.
The problem this creates is that we tend to value so-called 'positive' emotions and deny or denigrate the ones we consider to be 'negative.' Yet, *anger* has the purpose of alerting us to injustice, *jealousy* to the possibility that we may

lose a relationship, and *boredom* that we are engaged in something that has no value to us. The practice of suspending judgment and speculating on why an emotion is showing up when and where it does can help us respect and value all emotions as sources of information and guidance.

- **Interpretations.** We cannot see emotions directly. We can notice a person's posture, facial expression, or energy, and speculate on the emotions they are feeling, but we cannot be sure. A person's words or intonation when they speak are other clues, but they are not definitive. Even when we name our emotions we are interpreting sensations or thoughts to articulate them. The implication of this is that if we want to have a serious conversation about emotions, we need to first agree on a shared interpretation. We need to agree on the meaning and purpose of the emotion we are discussing. If we do not, we risk being in different conversations and thus unable to understand one another.

- **Logical.** While emotions may be "irrational," meaning they don't spring from reason or intellect alone, they are not "illogical." If something has a pattern we can identify and reproduce, it is logical. Emotions follow a pattern that includes:

  - **A consistent, underlying story or narrative:** Every emotion offers us information. We sometimes call this a belief, thought, perspective, or understanding. In any case, the narrative is what we are thinking when we feel an emotion. We may express it verbally, or we may not, but it is there in our thoughts. In *disappointment,* we realize something we hoped for or expected is not going to happen. When we experience *peace,* it is because we cannot imagine there is even a hint of danger. *Dissatisfaction* is connected with the story that something is lacking for us.

- **An impulse:** We feel moved to act in a certain way whether we do or not. We've learned to hit the pause button on some emotions in some circumstances. We don't generally express *joy* at a funeral or *despair* at a wedding, even if we feel like it. The value of noticing our impulse is that it informs us of the emotion we are experiencing.

- **A purpose:** Every emotion exists to allow us to do something we could not do without it. That does not mean we will like what every emotion allows us to do. *Rage* allows us to destroy without regard for the consequences because we believe nothing is worth saving. That generates pain, suffering, and hurt. Yet, without *rage,* we could not start over or eliminate things we consider evil. Not pretty, but necessary. The purposes of other emotions are more apparent. *Affection* draws us closer to others, *kindness* urges us to treat others as family or kin in the best sense of the word, and *compassion* to be with others when they are struggling or suffering.

Example: Imagine losing a person or thing you care about. It might be a partner or mentor in the agency, rank, a promotion, or going through a divorce. What emotion will you feel? Sadness. That's because sadness and the belief that *"I've lost something I care about"* always go together. Our impulse in sadness is to withdraw and be alone. The purpose of sadness is to highlight what we care about.

This pattern is consistent and universal, thus predictable and logical. We don't know when we'll lose something that holds importance for us, but we can be sure we'll feel the emotion of *sadness* when we do. It turns out that it isn't our emotions that are unpredictable, it is life. We've mislabeled the *uncertainty of life* as the *unpredictability of emotions*.

Emotions are both an individual and a collective experience

Because we can't directly see emotions, we sometimes make the error of believing that they function in the same way as our organs: self-contained and self-sufficient. Yet, we all have experienced times when the emotions of those around us affected ours.

We 'share' emotions with others in two ways. At times, we feel, and they feel, the same emotion; thus, we have that in common. At other times, we transfer or receive the energy of emotions from others. Have you ever walked into a meeting and the emotion of happiness and immediately felt that the emotion in the room was serious? What happened to you at that moment? Probably, without planning, you shifted into the prevailing emotion, and your contentment disappeared.

This aspect of emotions is one of the drivers for having your stadium full of cheering fans, organizing a large demonstration, or inviting two hundred guests to a wedding. Emotions are as much a collective experience as an individual one, which gives us the possibility of aligning the emotional energy of a team or organization.

Emotional Literacy vs Emotional Intelligence

These days, there is a lot of talk about the importance of being emotionally intelligent. You may have taken an assessment to measure your EQ. While that is important, having insight into your level of emotional intelligence does nothing to change or develop it.

Remember taking your first IQ test? It said something about your intellectual capacity and knowledge but didn't elevate or expand your intelligence. For that, you needed other tools. You needed literacy. You learned the alphabet, then to read and write. Those have helped you access and enhance your intellect. And what a job they've done!

Linguistic literacy is one of the primary competencies that allows humans to survive and grow. And it is something we now take for granted in many places.

Now, think about your EQ assessment. Whatever you know about your level of emotional intelligence may help you understand why you are good at some things and struggle with others, but understanding your EQ score does not change it. For that, you need the equivalent of linguistic literacy in the emotional domain. You need *emotional literacy*, which is the ability to notice, name, and navigate your emotions. You need tools and practice, not theory.

The relationship between IQ and linguistic literacy, and EQ and emotional literacy looks like this:

Linguistic literacy and emotional literacy

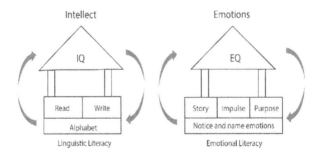

Knowing 'about' does not equal 'knowing how'

How has being an officer changed your view of policing? There is one view of being an officer on television and another view when you are on the street. You may know a lot about baseball, but that doesn't mean you can walk onto the stadium field and play with the pros. *Knowing about* and *knowing how* are different ways of knowing. Watching cooking shows doesn't make you a chef, going to see movies doesn't make you an actor, and knowing *about* emotions doesn't make you emotionally competent.

To master any discipline, you need both *knowing about* and *knowing how*. Knowing how requires practice. It is what produces embodied knowledge, something theory cannot do. In the world of emotions, that means you need to understand their structure, distinctions between similar emotions, the difference between emotions and moods, and many other aspects, *AND* you need practice. How do you maintain an emotion? How do you shift an emotion that is not serving you? How do you reel in an emotion that is a bit over the line, causing you to say or do things that are not what you intend? The more you practice these and others, the more emotions will become a set of tools you can put to work at the moment you need them. It is not the child who is taught about love, but the child who has experienced it that grows into a healthy, happy, well-adjusted adult. He or she does not just know 'about' love.

If you are serious about mastering emotions as a tool you need to fully commit to practice. That means accepting that emotions are part of your makeup as a human being, learning to suspend judgment of them, seeking to understand how others navigate their emotions, and trying out new methodologies for yourself.

Why emotions? They allow us to start, stop, regulate, and adapt

The importance of emotions is that they "put us into action." That doesn't mean they always move us forward. They can cause us to hesitate, avoid, disengage, or deny. Understanding which emotions generate specific impulses and leveraging them with intention is part of mastery.

Personal mastery might suggest gaining dominance over people or things. But mastery also means a high level of proficiency. A master craftsperson does not dominate his or her materials. Mastering the grill means developing the ability to turn out a perfect steak every time no matter what the conditions.

Masterful people are able to consistently generate the results that matter most deeply to them. They commit to lifelong learning. Personal mastery is the discipline of continually clarifying and deepening your personal vision, focusing your energies, developing patience, and honestly considering your limitations. You'll notice that emotions play a significant part in all of those.

If you are someone with easy access to *boldness,* you will probably jump into situations more quickly than others. It may show up in moments of urgency. Many times, that will be beneficial, but sometimes it may land you in trouble. And, if you are someone who tends to hesitate because *prudence* is one of your go-to emotions, a little *boldness* may be just the thing.

Humans are infinitely complex, and with hundreds of possible emotions that change by the second, mastery is a lifelong pursuit but one that is immeasurably rewarding. Many people believe that emotions are complex. In our view, emotions are straightforward, but we are wonderfully complex and unique beings. And that is as it should be.

Emotions as a life skill and competence

Abe Lincoln once said, "You cannot change human nature, but you can change human action." And the thing needed for that in the authors' experience is emotional self-knowledge. For a long time, we've thought of emotions as either extraneous or a "nice to have," but research is revealing more each day that emotions are at the root of all our relationship-building, decision-making, problem-solving, and our worldview.

Emotions, it turns out, are the prime mover in our lives. There is precious little, if anything, in our lives that isn't begun, guided, or shaped by emotions. Some examples:

There are specific emotions that determine:

- What we do: *Curiosity, boredom, wonder, passion, hate...*
- How we do it: *Service, compassion, impatience, kindness, boldness...*
- Why we do it: *Empathy, pity, respect, honor, affection...*
- Who we do it with: *Trust, loyalty, enjoyment, adventurousness, intrigue...*
- If we do it at all: *Enthusiasm, faith, complacency, obligation, dignity...*

Beyond that, there are sets of emotions that:

- Draw us closer to others: *Affection, admiration, curiosity, desire, kindness...*
- Distance us from others: *Suspicion, hate, disgust, uncertainty, distrust...*
- Give us a sense of strength: *Boldness, dignity, adventurousness, faith, boldness...*
- Expand our vision: *Enthusiasm, wonder, intrigue, inspiration, awe...*
- Narrow our vision: *Ambition, skepticism, urgency, anger, frustration...*

Emotions as a gift

Discovering the gift of emotions is life-changing. We discover that the ones we previously wanted to get rid of are there to serve us. We see that no matter what emotion "has us," we have the latitude to shift it to one that can be more helpful. We learn that planning future events using the lens of emotions can make them less stressful and more productive. We begin to see the richness of having more than 200 emotions, the incredible ways they interact with each other, and their influence on all aspects of our lives.

Nothing about emotions is "soft". As life skills, they are the real deal, and we dismiss them at our peril. When we connect emotions with our stories and beliefs, we see that there are emotions that help us think and act with more agility. We notice that resilience is not just a mental capability, but is, in large part, the ability to 'bounce back' to our emotional center. When we are intellectually resilient, it allows us to 'change our mind.' Emotions are thoughts that generate energy, and all an emotion wants to do is to be experienced. The stories we tell ourselves to the contrary only stop us from appreciating their value.

One of the biggest realizations you may have, if you dare think it, is that the domain of emotions is as broad and deep as the world of reason and intellect. Humans have, for several centuries, focused on intellectual development to the extent that we've come to believe that true knowledge resides in the brain and everything else is of lesser importance. Neuroscientific exploration into emotions is revealing that perhaps we've had it wrong. Maybe humans are not thinking beings who have emotions but are emotional beings that think, to paraphrase neuroscientist Antonio Damasio.

We don't have a position on or answer to that riddle, but what we can say with certainty from our experience is that a human being who develops themselves intellectually AND emotionally is more competent, well-rounded, and satisfied. You've done the intellectual learning, now is the time for emotional development.

Questions to ask yourself

- What did you learn about emotions while growing up that isn't serving you today?
- How could you see emotions in a more useful way?
- What beliefs about emotions would you need to let go of?
- How does staying within your emotional comfort zone protect you from potential discomfort or uncertainty, even if it prevents positive growth?
- How do emotions such as fear, anger, or sadness, contribute to your resistance to change?

Practical application

- Complete the following sentences for yourself. We encourage you to write out your answers. Seeing them on the page is more clarifying than simply thinking about them.

  - *"An emotion, to me, is…"*
  - *"Humans have emotions because…"*
  - *"The challenges of having emotions, for me, are…"*
  - *"The benefits of having emotions, for me, are…"*

Section 2:
What Has Been Missing

*"You can dodge your responsibilities, but you cannot
dodge the consequences of dodging your responsibilities".*

Chapter 5
Stop Looking out There….it is all in Here

"Each of us guards a gate of change that can only be opened from the inside."

- Marilyn Ferguson

Chapter bullets

- How emotions really work, but no one ever told you
- Building emotional agility and resilience
- Committing to emotional self-care and wellbeing

Story

A federal task force approached my Team requesting that we gather intelligence and make apprehensions on suspects that were part of a crime ring selling military weapons parts to a local gang in southern California. We were given three targets to surveil and plan for a high-risk warrant. We were given little to no information about the habits or even the whereabouts of these individuals other than the fact that they lived on our base and their names.

I broke the team into three groups and assigned each of them an individual to track and follow. For days, they followed and watched the patterns of the individuals. Once we had the information, we began a plan to apprehend the suspects. Many people, including the chain of command, wanted us to smash open the door, grab the suspects, and be home before dinner. My thoughts were that there was no reason to put my team at any risk when we could simply control the environment to reduce the risk.

55

Most of our suspects would work out in the morning with their units. It is very hard to carry a gun in workout clothes. The plan was simple: have a tail in place to notify us when they left their home in the morning, then follow them to our ambush location. Upon arrival at the parking lot of their workplace, we would quickly deploy, box them in and apprehend them.

At zero dark thirty, our entire team was staged and ready to go before the suspects were even awake. My team and I were at the staging point waiting for communication from our tail that there was movement. I noticed that the team was uptight and nervous at the unknown. I made a conscious effort to calm them down with humor and talking about their hobbies. Sounds too easy to believe, but if you can get someone to start talking about their hobbies, they will relax. Most people use hobbies to reduce stress and relax in their daily life. Talking about hobbies brings some of those same feelings. After a few laughs and some good discussion, the team was mentally prepared to carry out our mission. The rest is history.... of course, we got the bad guys without any trouble.

Dustin S., State Director/Peer Network

Why we have emotions

Emotions are not only unavoidable; they are desirable. We sometimes forget this in our effort to avoid the discomfort some bring. Without emotions that generate tension, we feel flat. We consciously or unconsciously seek out emotions that energize us - excitement, anticipation, even fear - because we feel alive when we experience them.

Many times, these and other emotions are the result of interactions rather than something we've chosen. When our lives are full of these types of interactions, the level of emotions we experience can become too much. We feel overwhelmed and exhausted by them, and that provokes other emotions like irritation, annoyance, or frustration.

All of us are born with the possibility of learning to navigate or moderate our emotions. We may call it emotional agility, emotional resilience, emotional regulation, or managing our emotions, but they all point to the same thing: **We have a lot of latitude in the way we live our emotions.** What is missing is that we've never been taught how.

How they work

Sometimes, the way we talk about emotions misrepresents what is truly happening. "The sun rises in the East and sets in the West". It may appear that way until you learn there is more to it than meets the eye.

When we say, "That person made me angry," we're implying that the other person has the power to control our emotions. Some other common misstatements include "she makes me happy" and "he makes me nervous."

If we look at how emotions work, we'll begin to see that those are not valid statements.

What is truly happening:

1. He or she did or said something (their action or inaction)
2. I have a story or belief about what that means (my interpretation)
3. My story generates an emotion

Here's an example that you've probably experienced first-hand:

Real-life example:

1. My sergeant said my report was not very long.
2. My interpretation was that he/she thought it was insufficient
3. That generated the emotion of ***embarrassment*** ("I feel like hiding")

Same experience, alternate story:

1. My sergeant said my report was not very long.
2. My interpretation was that he/she thought my report was concise
3. That generated the emotion of ***pride*** ("I did a good thing")

You can test this idea for yourself. Ask someone to "make you happy" or to "make you angry." If you monitor your story about what they say, you'll find that nothing they can do or say will automatically produce either happiness or anger. What would happen if you approached this with the assumption of positive intent? Emotions are within you and belong to you.

What this tells us is that if we want to master our emotions and empower ourselves emotionally, we need to claim our emotions as our responsibility and do the internal work to learn all we can about them. Here are some beginning concepts to work on.

Emotional agility

To be agile means to be nimble and quick, to be able to shift while maintaining your balance. Imagine the best football player you can remember zig-zagging through the other team's defense, never slowing their forward progress. That is an example of what agility looks like physically. Imagine that you could do the same thing emotionally.

It is not unusual to get stuck in strong emotions like anxiety, anger, or doubt. While those emotions have a purpose and show up initially to tell us something or guide us, once they've "done their work," it may be more productive to shift them.

The problem for many of us is that we never learned how to move from one emotion to another by choice. In fact, many people believe it is not possible and that we need to "wait it out," "cool down," or "process" emotions before they will shift.

While there are certain physiological changes we cannot choose at will, there is a process for selecting emotions and moving from one to another. This is called emotional navigation and is at the core of emotional agility. If you can't wait to find out how to create an emotional shift, skip ahead to chapter 11.

Emotional resilience

Think about physical balance. Imagine you trip on the sidewalk. You've lost your balance. Recovering it requires physical strength, orientation, and flexibility. You may stumble forward, but that is part of regaining your balance and bouncing back. Once you are re-centered physically, you can continue on your way.

How are you at "bouncing back" when an experience provokes a strong emotional reaction in you? Is the recovery happening easily and quickly? Can you maintain awareness of your reaction and response simultaneously? You will react, but will that resolve the issue? What is your strategy for generating an appropriate response?

,tional resilience is the intelligent regulation of emotions. It ,e combined strength of your intellect and your emotions to recenter, not either/or.

When you notice resentment rising, do you automatically ask yourself what you consider unfair? Once done, can you select an emotion that would be more helpful than resentment? Curiosity, perhaps, or acceptance, tolerance, or compassion? What is your practice to shift emotions intentionally?

In every moment of every day, we are engaged in experiences that provoke emotions. *Event > interpretation > emotion*. Some of the emotions we experience are pleasant and enjoyable, some are distressing. Whichever it is, the value of emotional resilience is that if the emotion pushes us off balance, we can quickly and effortlessly return to our emotional center.

Emotional self-care

Pythons swallow their prey whole and digest it over a long period of time while immobile. Humans are not built to nourish themselves in that way. From the python's point of view, we eat small meals, often, and digest on the go.

Every system has limits for input and output. In the case of human emotional capacity, when the system gets overwhelmed, the flow stops. If input continues, but there is not sufficient resolution or flow-thru, the system gets overwhelmed and stops functioning.

What causes the slowdown in our "emotional digestion"? Many of the myths and misconceptions we've already talked about. In addition, we may attempt to avoid emotions, judge emotions, or believe we shouldn't talk about them. Many of these are or include brain functions. The brain does its best, but sometimes it misleads us because it doesn't know better.

Denial and Suppression

Denial is an emotion that allows us to ignore our emotions when they are too intense or uncomfortable. In denial, we believe that if we don't pay attention, the demon will go away. It won't, but that is what we believe. Denial has its purpose but casts a long shadow. When we ignore the hard problems, the hard problems do not go away and often get worse.

Emotional suppression is a phenomenon in law enforcement that allows you to set aside reacting because you have to maintain control of the scene, call, or situation. It is a coping strategy in which an individual consciously attempts to inhibit or hide their emotional responses. It can include masking emotions with a neutral or different expression. It is not the same as denial; however, habitual suppression can lead to increased stress and difficulty in interpersonal relationships, as it hinders genuine emotional expression and connection.

So, what is the difference between emotional suppression and emotional regulation? Well, they both are ways of managing your emotions.

By contrast, emotional regulation is a healthy and adaptive process during which an individual acknowledges, understands, and modulates their emotional responses in a balanced and appropriate manner. It is the ability to experience a range of emotions without being overwhelmed by them, and to express them in a socially acceptable and constructive way. Emotional regulation is an essential skill for maintaining emotional well-being and forming authentic, positive relationships with others. The good news is that emotional regulation is a skill that can be learned by us all.

Emotional self-care is not something you do once in a while. It is a way of being. It is like breathing. You can't stop breathing for any length of time and expect to survive. Emotional self-care requires that we reflect on and resolve emotions as we go. We need techniques that include paying attention to them, reflecting on their purpose, understanding their messages or meaning, and the ability to strengthen emotions that support us.

We have a choice in our approach to physical health. We can pay attention to our well-being and act in ways that support it, or we can ignore it and assume that we'll be able to repair it when we fall ill. Emotional self-care allows emotional hygiene, which is the practice of taking care of your emotions with the same diligence as you do to take care of your body (or know you should). This is the difference between healthcare and medical attention.

We are talking about emotional well-being because no one can take care of your emotions for you. Only you can decide if you are worth the learning it will take and the commitment to the practices required to remain emotionally well, agile, and resilient. As you can see, the above is "all the time work." All the time, work allows us to be jolted and not destroyed when calamity hits.

The potential for all of these emotional competencies exists within us, or they don't...*yet*. They are skills only we can nurture and develop. No one can do it for us. Practice is the mother of all skills.

Emotional well-being

There is a lot of talk about the need for mental health support in policing. Agencies are implementing programs and encouraging participation. This is both compassionate and honorable. However, there is confusion about what mental health is, how it relates to emotional well-being, and how we achieve or safeguard it.

The World Health Organization (WHO) conceptualizes mental health as a "state of well-being in which the individual realizes his or her own abilities, can cope with the normal stresses of life, can work productively and fruitfully, and is able to make a contribution to his or her community."

One element of confusion is the use of the word "mental." That provokes the idea that the well-being the WHO visualizes can be achieved intellectually. The authors disagree. If, as we've argued, thoughts stem from or are co-creative with emotions, then building emotional capacity will have a direct impact on generating well-being and mental health.

"Emotions are basic features of human functioning. As such, they play a key role in both mental health and illness throughout the entire lifespan: maladaptive emotional functioning is thought to be a critical feature in nearly all mental disorders. Definitions of emotional functioning vary, but all note that emotional functioning entails the experience, expression, and regulation of positive and negative emotions as well as symptoms of emotional problems such as anxiety, depression, and aggressive behavior". This is according to Frontiers, the 3rd most-cited and 6th largest research publisher and open science platform globally.

The authors believe it is time to demystify mental health to reduce the stigma often associated with it and to help people realize that they can prepare themselves better to face the stresses and challenges of life by embracing their emotions.

Questions to ask yourself

- What are situations in which you give away your emotional power?
- Who are people to whom you give away your emotional power?
- What is keeping you from taking ownership and responsibility for your emotions?
- What would be the first step?

- Are there any past experiences rooted in emotions that have shaped your resistance to emotional change?

Practical application

- **Elevate emotional awareness:** Have a conversation with your staff about what is being asked of them, what emotions it provokes, and how those emotions will impact execution of the task, whether for better or worse.
- **Emotional Intelligence Professional Development:** Provide comprehensive training programs that focus on emotional intelligence development for first responders. These programs can include working sessions, simulations, and scenario-based training to enhance self-awareness, empathy, emotional regulation, and communication skills.
- **Regular Mental Health Check-ins:** Implement routine mental health check-ins for officers to create a safe space for them to express their emotions, concerns, and challenges. This can be done through confidential conversations with mental health professionals or designated departmental personnel trained in providing emotional support.
- **Leadership Role Modeling:** Encourage departmental leaders, supervisors, and commanders to lead by example in promoting emotional well-being. When leaders openly prioritize and demonstrate emotional intelligence, it sets a positive tone and encourages first responders to engage in their own emotional growth. People are a product of their past life experiences and the sum total of their role models. People do what people see. We can all be role models to the skill model.

Chapter 6
Right Decisions Require the Right Emotions

"Don't do something permanently stupid because you're temporarily upset."

- Zig Ziglar

Chapter bullets

- Key emotions in policing
- Emotions that generate stress
- Emotions that diminish stress

Story

As I drove to the house, I wondered how this call was going to go. Like all 'bad' calls, this one came in the early morning hours. As a major city police department's senior chaplain, being on call in case one of our officers was injured or died in the line of duty was just part of the job. I knew the response to this particular call would be more difficult in that not only did it deal with the suicide of a former officer, but the spouse of this former officer was also a highly respected officer with our agency.

The former officer had tried to evade law enforcement officers from another city and then took his life as they approached the vehicle. I knew this officer had left the agency to avoid the consequences of his long-term issues with alcoholism shortly after going through a bitter divorce. After cutting all ties with family and friends, this officer decided on a "permanent solution to a temporary problem".

As I waited for someone to answer the door, I wondered how we got there. What was the cause? Was it grieving over the demise of a marriage? Was it lamenting the loss of a career? Was it the erosion of hope? Whatever the cause, the fact was this former officer had been psychologically vetted before he was hired. He was judged to be mentally sound and to have the appropriate personality strengths to do the job. So, what happened?

The answer is found not just in a career's worth of traumatizing calls and living with almost constant stress. This one impulsive, irrational, totally devastating act was the result of an abundance of bad decisions resulting from living with destructive emotions that were not regulated in a healthy way. The lack of emotional awareness and constructive self-regulation in this case was more than problematic. It left three children without a father and an entire police agency, wondering if there was something we could have done that would have prevented this tragedy.

Rick R., Chaplain

So, how is it possible to predict a first responder's healthy goal of protecting and serving and prevent it from escalating into unhealthy hypervigilant behavior? Is there a way to accurately measure how someone makes decisions, solves problems, and builds relationships to bridge the gap between the protected and the protectors, and thereby enhance community engagement? How do we find the balance for first responders to be both successful (high-performing) and well-adjusted (emotionally fit)? And finally, what does a high-performing, emotionally fit first responder for the 21st Century look like?

Key emotions in policing

If we define emotions using the criteria that each has a unique story, a specific impulse, and a purpose, there are more than 200. All are equally important, but not all are experienced with the same frequency. Life situations often dictate the emotions one experiences frequently.

The following is a short list of emotions you may experience regularly in your work. Understanding them is the first step to mastering them:

Emotion	Story/Belief	Impulse	Purpose	Impact
Anxiety	*"I believe there may be danger but am not sure of the source"*	To remain vigilant	To keep you vigilant for possible danger from an unknown source	Keeps us vigilant to possible danger but can become a habitual emotion we turn to whenever we feel discomfort
Dignity	*"I believe I have inherent worth and am equal to all other humans"*	To take a stand for what we believe	To set and protect our personal boundaries	Allows us to take care of ourselves as only we can, but it may be seen as arrogance or selfishness by others
Dispassion	*"I choose to set aside my emotions for this moment"*	To operate more from reason than emotions	Allows you to be less influenced by the emotions of the moment	Allows us to be pragmatic or practical while not emotionless but can be interpreted by others as being cold
Doubt	*"I'm unsure because this is new to me"*	To prepare	To be sure we prepare and don't assume we know	Focuses our energy on preparation but cannot be eliminated. We must act for it to be resolved
Empathy	*"I feel your pain"*	To feel what the other is feeling	To let another person know that you understand what they are experiencing	Creates a primal emotional connection with another human, but in excess, it can exhaust us
Fear	*"I perceive there might be danger"*	To avoid harm	To keep you safe	Keep us safe from specific danger but can become a mood that causes us to see the world as dangerous.
Frustration	*"This is slower or more difficult than I expected"*	To look for new possibilities that speed things up	To redirect you to more streamlined ways of doing things	Prompts us to look for simpler, faster methods, but it can be interpreted as something being wrong.

Emotion	Story/Belief	Impulse	Purpose	Impact
Loyalty	*"I will defend my group"*	To protect others I feel connected to	To defend a group we feel we are a part of	Is the glue that holds groups together but can be misdirected or abused.
Passion	*"I want to be a part this"*	To immerse ourselves	Unites us with others with similar interests or cares	Engages us with others at the deepest level but can be confused with other inappropriate emotions.
Perseverance	*"There is a way"*	To continue looking for a way	Keeps us searching for possible solutions	Keeps us engaged and seeking a way to succeed but can exhaust us when we do not have the means to rein it in.
Pride	*"I did something good"*	To appreciate ourselves or our accomplishments	To help us acknowledge the good in us or that we've done	Celebrates our goodness in being or deeds but can be confused with smugness or arrogance.
Tolerance	*"I will endure"*	To put up with an uncomfortable situation	To help us get through difficulties	Let's us endure situations that we cannot accept but can morph into obligation or resentment.
Trust	*"I am safe"*	To interact freely	To allow us to coordinate action with an appropriate level of risk	Allows us to interact with others but may be confused with a guarantee of safety when it is not.
Urgency	*"It must happen now"*	To act immediately	To generate immediate action	Moves us to act without hesitation but generates significant stress that may be unsustainable.

Whichever emotions you have available at the moment of choice are the emotions that will generate your actions. Richard Strozzi, a teacher of ours, proposes that it isn't the case that we rise to the occasion. What happens is that we sink to the level of our practices. We agree.

Every decision is driven by an emotion

A legal duty for first responders to intervene if they witness another first responder misbehave has been around for more than 50 years. More recently, however, in response to a number of viral, wrenching police non-interventions, the concept has been the subject of more court decisions, codified in more state and local laws and ordinances, and incorporated into more law enforcement policies.

The vexing question is how to de-escalate a situation that is starting to cross the line from rigorous policing to abuse. From the authors' perspective, these situations don't develop because anyone thinks they are a good idea. No one starts with the intention to treat people badly, yet that is what sometimes occurs. Situations can cascade into horrible regrets.

Duty to Intervene training attempts to prepare police to handle themselves honorably in challenging situations. They focus on the way first responders think and react to intense situations, but extend to many other areas, including report writing, good faith mistakes, and health and wellness matters.

Years of academic research and on-the-ground experience have shown us that effective active bystandership can be taught and learned. The Center for Innovations in Community Safety, partnering with global law firm Sheppard Mullin, has created Project ABLE® (Active Bystandership for Law Enforcement) to prepare officers to successfully intervene to prevent harm and to create a law enforcement culture that supports peer intervention.

Growing out of a small program created in New Orleans in 2016 by a group of forward-thinking police officers, community stakeholders, and psychologists, the ABLE Project has become a national hub for training, technical assistance, and research, all with the aim of creating a police culture in which officers routinely intervene - and accept interventions - as necessary to:

- Prevent misconduct
- Reduce law enforcement mistakes
- Promote officer health and wellness

As of September 2023, more than 350 law enforcement agencies across the U.S. and Canada had joined the ABLE program, representing more than 196,000 officers. These officers are responsible for serving more than 97,000,000 community members. In that same period, ABLE has trained more than 2,000 law enforcement officers as ABLE-certified instructors.

Adding emotions to the mix

There are specific emotions that both support interventions and others that create barriers. The missing piece we're suggesting, that emotions are the filter between training and behavior, shows their impact when applied to duty to intervene situations.

When an officer is witnessing a situation that calls for intervention, her or his action depends not just on their training, but also on their competence to act from the emotions that will generate the desired outcome. They need the capacity to choose emotionally as well as rationally.

While procedures such as duty to intervene are, in the authors' view, essential and well-intentioned, they have traditionally left out the critical role of emotions in moments of choice. A key strength of the ABLE program is that it includes the essential role of emotions to enable intervention when needed.

Furthermore, there is one emotion inherent to and hidden inside most procedures and rules. Obligation. It means you have no choice - or at least perceive that you have no choice - about whether to follow and implement the procedure or not. You must.

When officers are conflicted - i.e., when their culture tells them they should comply, but their training or moral code tells them they should resist, or vice versa - it generates significant emotional uncertainty.

key wording and confirmation in this section were generously provided by Jonathan Aronie, Co-Founder of the ABLE Project and Chair of the ABLE Project Board of Advisors.

The following models show the impact of the officer's emotion at the moment of choice:

Emotion example: Anger

| Competence: "Duty to Intervene Training" | > | Emotion: Anger - "This is unjust or morally wrong" | > | Action: Desire to Punish the citizen, thus not intervening |

71

Emotion example: Disdain

Competence:
" Duty to Intervene Training "

Emotion:
Disdain - " They're not worth my time"

Action:
Treat the citizen as worthless which might appear as not intervening

Emotion example: Compassion

Competence:
" Duty to Intervene Training "

Emotion:
Compassion - "I want to understand this person"

Action:
Intervening because you want to, first and foremost, understand the situation

Emotion example: Honor

Competence:
" Duty to Intervene Training "

Emotion:
Honor - " I choose to do what I believe is right "

Action:
Intervening because you believe it is the right thing to do

Learning and practicing emotions is the path to creating the filter that will serve you in times of stress and peace.

On the street

On January 10, 2023, Tyre Nichols was tragically killed by 5 members of the Memphis Police Department/SCORPION Unit. This was a select group of 50 officers originally formed to fight violent street crime. Tadarrius Bean, Demetrius Haley, Justin Smith, Emmitt Martin III, and Desmond Mills, Jr. are all charged with one count of second-degree murder, aggravated assault-acting in concert, two counts of aggravated kidnapping, two counts of official misconduct and one count of official oppression.

A central Florida man died after a 911 trainee sent the ambulance to the wrong address while a colleague who was supposed to be supervising them was instead on her cell phone, according to officials.

Imagine how the outcome might have been different if the police professionals had been operating with a higher level of emotional competence, agility, and resilience…supervised by respect and dignity.

Ten Emotions That Generate Stress

Stress is a phenomenon that exists in both living and nonliving parts of nature. It is what allows muscles to function, suspension bridges to exist, and plants to grow vertically. It is not positive or negative. When stress exceeds the limits of a system it becomes strain. Strain is the point at which damage to the system begins.

Stress is not a single emotion but is generated by a wide variety of them. Some of these emotions we think of as positive, like *ambition* and *excitement*. Remember our proposal that we reconsider emotions as neither positive or negative. Others that generate stress we consider to be negative, but they nonetheless have a purpose and support us in their way.

If we want to understand the stress we are experiencing, we need to look for the emotion or emotions that are generating it. Likewise, in the second table, we can look for emotions that will relax or diminish stress when it is valuable to do so.

Emotions that generate or contribute to our stress level

Emotions	Etymological root	What we think or say	Our reaction or impulse for action is...	Its purpose is to...
Anger	Latin *angere*, "to throttle, torment"	"This is wrong or unjust."	To punish the source of injustice	Identify injustice and, by extension, justice
Anxiety	From Latin *anxius*, "solicitous, uneasy, troubled in mind," figuratively "torment, cause distress"	"I believe something may harm me, but I'm not sure what it might be."	To worry	Warn us of possible danger even if we can't identify the source.
Confusion	From Latin *confusionem*, "a mingling, mixing, blending, disorder," and *confundere* "to pour together"	"This doesn't match my understanding."	Try to figure out how a new idea fits into our worldview	Make sense of things that aren't part of our current understanding
Dread	Late 12c., a shortening of Old English *adrædan*, "counsel or advise against"	"I can't face this."	To avoid, if possible, or proceed with utmost caution	Avoid what we fear
Fear	From Old English *fær*, "calamity, sudden danger, peril, sudden attack"	"I believe something may harm me, and I know what it is."	To avoid perceived danger	Help us avoid danger
Frustration	From Latin *frustrationem*, "a deception, a disappointment"	"It should've already happened; it shouldn't be this hard."	To look for a faster or simpler way	Challenge us to find a simpler or faster way
Impatience	Latin *in-* "not," + *patientia*, "endurance, submission"	"I am ready, but others are not."	To look for a way around whatever is blocking us	Get into action
Surprise	From *sur-* "over" + *prendre* "to take," from Latin *prendere*, contracted from *prehendere* "to grasp, seize"	"I didn't expect that!"	To momentarily disbelieve	Inform us when something unexpected has happened

Emotions	Etymological root	What we think or say	Our reaction or impulse for action is...	Its purpose is to...
Uncertainty	From Vulgar Latin *certanus*, from Latin *certus,* "sure, fixed, settled, determined" + *un* "not"	"I'm not sure which option is the better one."	To hesitate	Tell us when the path to take is not clear
Urgency	From Latin *urgentem*, "to press hard"	"It needs to be done now!"	Move very rapidly	Take care of emergencies

Emotions that help release or diminish stress

Emotions	Etymological root	What we think or say	Our reaction or impulse for action is…	Its purpose is to…
Acceptance	From Latin *acceptare,* "take or receive willingly"	"It is so even though I may not agree, endorse, or like it."	To be at peace with what is	Help us align with present reality
Appreciation	Late Latin *appretiatus,* "to set a price to"	"This is of value to me."	To thank	Show us what has value for us
Compassion	Latin *compassionem,* from *com-* "together" + *pati* "to suffer"	"I'm with you in your challenges."	To be with another in his/her difficulty or pain	Be with others in their pain or struggle
Curiosity	From Latin *curiositatem,* "desire of knowledge, inquisitiveness"	"Tell me more."	Seek more information	Keep us learning, engaged in life, and looking for new possibilities
Dignity	From Latin *dignitatem,* "worthiness," and *dignus,* "worth, worthy, proper, fitting"	"I am worthy; I decide."	To act as a legitimate human being deserving of respect	Set and protect personal boundaries
Equanimity	from Latin *aequanimitatem,* "evenness of mind, calmness; goodwill, kindness"	"I feel balanced, centered, and able to look at all sides of the situation."	To consider in a calm and even-handed manner	Allow us to consider things from a balanced emotional state
Faith	From Latin *fides,* "trust, reliance, credence, belief"	"I believe it even though I don't have any evidence it is true."	To commit to a belief	Allow us to believe without relying on evidence

Emotions that help release or diminish stress

Emotions	Etymological root	What we think or say	Our reaction or impulse for action is...	Its purpose is to...
Gratitude	From Latin *gratia*, "favor, esteem, regard; pleasing quality, goodwill"	"Life and everything that is a part of it is a gift."	To appreciate all that I've received for free	Make us realize that even life is a gift and not something we have earned or perhaps even deserve
Irreverence	Latin *irreverentia*, "want of reverence," from revereri, "to stand in awe of, respect, honor, fear, be afraid of"	"I can make light of this even though it is a serious topic."	To take lightly	Let us be light-hearted even in serious matters
Tenderness	From Latin *tenerem*, "soft, delicate; of tender age, youthful"	"You are safe." "It will be alright."	To provide safety for others	Allow us to provide a sense of safety to others

If you compare these two tables, one thing you'll notice is that the majority of the first list are part of a typical police working day, and few from the second list are.

What that points to is that your work will, by its nature, generate emotional stress that needs to be released or counterbalanced. That is essential so that the stress you experience each day does not congeal into chronic stress. If you do not have access to the emotions that allow you to relax and unwind emotionally, how will you?

Many typical 'remedies' will divert you from stress, but don't resolve it. Drinking, social media, hobbies, or working more are not the answers you need. They help you ignore the emotions that generate stress, but they do not alleviate them. That requires strengthening the emotions in the second table, which in turn requires learning and practice.

Your emotions need your attention and care if they are going to care for you.

Questions to ask yourself

- When you complain about stress, are you more accurately talking about strain?
- What emotions are the biggest stress producers for you?
- What emotions could you practice and strengthen that would allow you to counterbalance the stresses you regularly experience?

Practical application

- **Establish Boundaries:** Create a clear balance between your work and personal life to ensure time for relaxation, self-care, rejuvenation, and belonging. Prioritize activities and relationships outside of work that contribute to your emotional well-being.
- **Develop Healthy Coping Mechanisms:** Identify healthy coping mechanisms that work best for you, such as physical activity, helping others, listening to music, or journaling. Engaging in activities that bring joy and other emotions that promote relaxation and restore emotional balance.
- **Notice and name:** Develop self-awareness by recognizing and acknowledging the presence of stressful emotions as they arise. Pay attention to your physical sensations, thoughts, and behavioral cues that indicate stress then keep a written record. Notice the frequency and patterns of your emotions.

Chapter 7
They're Called "Your Emotions" for a Reason

"When it comes to emotional regulation, nobody can do it for you."

Chapter bullets

- Self-empowerment requires taking responsibility for your emotions
- Shifting emotions with intentionality
- Emotional practice is the only thing that will get you there

Story

"Is what we do more important than how we do it?" Countless times, day first responders are faced with that question. "Is what I am about to do more important than how I get it done?" Often, we work through the issues of the day without noticing how we actually completed the work. For example, every shift, we are called to help someone on their worst day with the intent of helping them get their life back on track. Time and time again, we show up, fix the issue, and leave. We do this without thinking about our own emotions and generally don't acknowledge them. We simply show up and begin to add structure and resolution to the chaos.

But who does that for us? Who is responsible for showing up during our worst day to provide structure and resolution? If we're not careful with how we respond emotionally, we may derail our own lives.

Policing requires us to become emotionally aware of ourselves. We must understand that getting the job done requires just as much attention to how we do it as what we do. We don't get to choose the calls we go to; we do, however, get to choose how we show up.

Our emotions are the one thing we have full knowledge of and, with practice, full control. What an advantage! Police officers have the advantage of responding to calls with the training and understanding that the emotions they use are up to them. We have all seen officers not being aware of their emotions, and increasingly, it has led to the end of good careers.

I can't tell an officer how they should respond emotionally; that is uniquely up to them. It is what makes police departments great at what we do. We can't and shouldn't all be the same, or we will all choose the same response, which is sometimes wrong. If a police department wants to go far, they must go together. It takes creating an environment in which emotions aren't hidden, pushed away, and ignored. It takes practice for you to learn and for your team to live. We have to create "emotional backup" just as we do with tactical response. They are called 'your emotions,' but countless others depend on them. When it comes to emotional regulation, no one can do it for you.

Samuel G., Police Chief

Knowing minus action does not equal Not Knowing

Awareness is a two-edged sword. On the one hand, lack of awareness is a kind of blindness to what is, but if you cannot see something, you cannot act on it. Becoming aware carries with it a responsibility to determine how you will act. It does not automatically make you responsible for fixing it, but you can no longer ignore that you have a choice to make. Knowing – Action ≠ Not Knowing.

Taking responsibility – "You break it, you've bought it"

Now that you know that you are an emotional being, that emotions are part of your makeup, that they are your emotions, and you are responsible for what you do with them, you must decide what that will be. Will you deny or ignore what you've learned and continue as you always have? Or will you claim ownership and responsibility and learn about them? The fundamental question is, "What relationship will you choose to have with your emotions from this moment forward?"

Change is an inside job

Until now, you may have imagined you were moving from 'thought to action' without involving your emotions. Whether you were aware of it or not, your emotions always played a part. It may have been in *denying* what you felt, saw, or believed, or it may have been *hoping* that someone else would fix the problem.

Now you've seen how thoughts and emotions are co-creative and how they team up to determine your actions. You're aware that every emotion has the potential to support you or can be a barrier, depending on the situation. You've seen that when you are stuck in an emotion, you can learn the necessary tools to shift to a more helpful emotion.

Transforming theory into habit

Up to this point, we've covered an array of ideas and concepts. As long as they remain ideas, they are of limited value. It is time we began to investigate how to move from theory to practice. How do you use all of this to create a way of living that satisfies you?

Every human has three major ways of learning and knowing. We have intellect, which allows us to think, plan, assess, distinguish, evaluate, and understand. We have a body that allows us to sense, act and react.

And we have emotions that connect our brains with our bodies and translate between the two.

How we learn

The vast majority of formal education is based on developing our intellect. That has achieved marvelous things and given us enormous possibilities; however, it has limitations.

Think back to the time you learned to ride a bicycle. Your intellect helped you understand how a bicycle was ridden, which was translated to action by an emotion like *excitement*, and your body had to learn to balance, pedal, and steer all at the same time. The more you rode, the greater your skill became. You added new insights intellectually, integrated a few more emotions into the mix, like *prudence* or *boldness*, and increasingly refined your physical movements.

Three domains of learning

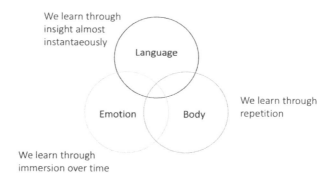

There are many learning theories, but from a practical perspective, it would appear that all learning includes these three domains: Language (the tool of intellect), emotions, and body.

If we consider those three aspects of every human, it is evident that, just as all three are present in everything we do, change requires that we include all three. Here is an illustration of the changes necessary in each if we want to shift an emotion we are experiencing:

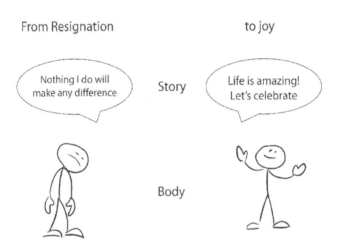

Every emotion has a consistent narrative: something we are thinking, a belief, or a story. The figure on the left has the story that "nothing I do will make any difference". That narrative is consistent with the emotion of *resignation*. In contrast, the figure on the right is thinking, "This is good and merits celebration". That aligns with the emotion of *joy*. Every emotion has this type of consistent internal narrative, no matter what is occurring externally. That means that when we change what we think we cannot remain in the emotion it generated.

Every emotion also generates a body that supports it. That can include our posture/stance, inclination, flexibility/rigidity, openness/closedness, tension/relaxation, a tilt of the head, breath, and facial expression, along with other visual cues and everything we are sensing internally. One helpful analogy is that the body is a container for the emotion.

You can see in the illustration that the body of *resignation* includes slumped shoulders, a collapsed chest, slack muscles, downcast eyes, inward focus, a frowning face, etc. In contrast, the body of *joy* is open, energetic, outwardly focused, with arms raised, face smiling, and eyes wide. The implication is that if we shift aspects of our body, it will begin to generate a different emotion. When we learn to shift intentionally, we can choose the emotion we'd like to generate.

What do we do when an emotion shows up without an invitation? Our reflex is sometimes to try to get rid of it. The problem with that is that we are still feeding it or giving it attention. When *jealousy* shows up, trying to push it away is not an effective solution. Many of us have learned that the "cure" for *fear* is *courage*. It can be, but there are other possibilities. The emotion you are looking for is the one that will allow you to "move through *fear*," not eliminate it.

If you consider the full range of possible emotions, you will find several that might allow this shift. This is not a one-size-fits-all situation, so no one can tell you what will work best for you. It might be *adventurousness, faith, dignity,* or another emotion. Whichever it is, that is your destination emotion and the one that you can focus on strengthening as a balancing emotion to your fear.

"Practice is the only thing that will convert theory to habit."

Converting practice into habit

This is no surprise to anyone. Want to be a competent softball pitcher? Practice. Want to dance without embarrassing yourself? Practice. Want to cook well? Practice. Want to be a better partner? Practice. Want to master your emotions? Practice.

Nothing we can say will make you practice. If you choose not to, the journey is over. You've gotten some new ideas, theories, and catchy expressions, but your emotional growth from here will be accidental and random. If you're satisfied as you are, *complacent,* emotionally speaking, here you'll stay.

However, if you are *dissatisfied, excited, inspired, hopeful, curious,* or *yearning* to understand yourself and others better, practice is the next step.

Questions to ask yourself

- What are examples of moments you have avoided taking responsibility for your emotions?
- When you've avoided responsibility for your emotions, how did things turn out?
- What is the connection between avoiding responsibility for your emotions and blame?
- What emotions would you like to cultivate or strengthen so they are more readily available?

Practical application

- Shifting an emotion:

    1. Notice what you are experiencing. What do you feel? What are you thinking?
    2. Name the emotion it represents to you.
    3. Ask yourself if the emotion you named is serving you or acting as a barrier. If it is serving you, great! If you decide it is not, it's time to shift!
    4. Imagine or search for an emotion that would serve you better. Check the list.
    5. Consider what your narrative/story/belief needs to change to.

6. Bodily, feel the first emotion and exaggerate it. Slowly reshape yourself to your chosen emotion while repeating the destination emotion's story. Feel the difference.

7. Now, practice, practice, practice. Commit to focusing on these steps several times a day. Find a safe place, set a schedule, and be intentional.

- Planning a challenging conversation:

    1. Think of an upcoming conversation and think about which emotion you would approach it in by default.
    2. Ask yourself whether that is the optimal emotion to get the results you want.
    3. If so, great, go have the conversation.
    4. If not, what emotion would serve you better?
    5. Name it, embody it, and find the narrative that creates it for you.
    6. Practice, practice, practice.

Section 3:
Program of Action

Chapter 8
Behaving our Way into Emotional Maturity

"To be mature means to face, and not evade, every fresh crisis that comes."

- Fritz Kunkel

Chapter bullets

- You can know the problem, you can know the solution, but it is only through a program of action that you start to see growth.
- Being a beginner requires self-compassion and perseverance.
- Where the focus goes, the energy flows.

Story

Do the Work

There is a parable of a wise man. He dug down deep to lay the foundation of his house on the rock. And when the torrent came, his house stood firm. What did that man look like? Sweat-covered, caked with dirt, calloused hands – but also steady, determined, and humble. A man who knew his need. A man who knew what he didn't have and that he had to dig down deep to find it because he knew the storm would surely come, and he wanted his house to stand. He got to work.

One of my favorite books is the historical fiction novel Gates of Fire by Steven Pressfield. It is the story of King Leonidas and the Spartan 300 at Thermopylae. There is a scene in this book where the Greeks arrive at the Hot Gates and need to rebuild a defensive wall. The engineers gather and draw plans in the dirt about how best to do that. They begin to argue amongst themselves about their possible courses of action. Until they look up and see what Leonidas, the king, has begun doing. Without a word or a command, he has started picking up stones, stacking them, one by one. Soon, every man is doing the same. There was no place for ego, just the immediacy of doing the work so that when the storm came, all could withstand it.

These aren't "my" stories, but they are my lessons. My Faith, Family, Friends, Department, Shift, Squad, Leadership, City. How do I protect these gifts? How do I honor them? I must remember that humility ceases to be a virtue when it hinders us from performing a required task. When it stops us short of getting to work. I must know (IQ) the need (EQ), lean into it, put my shoulder to the wheel, and get to work.

Dan and Marcel are about to ask us to do just that with a "Program of Action". These chapters show us the way but won't do the work for us. We have already started. You and I are in this book. We have started to pick up the stones, started to build, started to dig down. Why? So we can be the leaders that those we strive to honor and protect deserve to have. So we can be present, both physically and emotionally. And when the storm comes, we have built something that will stand, not just for ourselves, but for all who rely on us. That is the man I want to be in every aspect of my life. Let's dig down, lift the stones, do the work.

Sean B., Lieutenant

You Can't Give What You Don't Have

Marcel works in the psychometrics industry, which offers people insight into the science behind their identity and behavior. In other words, he measures how people problem-solve, make decisions, and build relationships when they are in their best day persona, their typical day persona, and their overextended/stressed persona.

New brain research and better technology allow us to measure how natural it is for a person to be impulsive, skeptical, unabashed, stoical, self-developing, contemplative, self-doubting, emotionally intelligent, self-scrutinizing, self-accepting, tough-minded, people-pleasing, hasty, or diplomatic, to name a few characteristics. We can now measure how naturally people "kick down and kiss up." This merger of human psychology and computer-assisted measurement techniques reveals who we are and how we interact with others through a new lens.

Here are a few things this new psychometric awareness allows us to see:

- You can't give what you don't have. If you have never learned how to be empathic, or you believe feeling empathy is a weakness, it won't be available when it is needed or would be useful.
- Behaviors that occur when you are overextended can now be measured. Sometimes, these behaviors can save your life, and sometimes, they require you to find a way to apologize. Overextended behavior occurs automatically and unconsciously in a fraction of a second.
- When overextended and not conscious of your emotions, you are at their mercy, and they dictate your behavior for better or worse.
- Ego and awareness cannot sit side-by-side. Self-awareness is the meta-skill for the 21st Century. Metacognition, or the ability to think about what you think about, allows you to observe how you are thinking, feeling, and behaving, and it is the new standard for all of us. We can become an observer of our thoughts.
- You can no longer say, "Well, this is just the way I am," and set the bar at zero in terms of growth. Research clearly shows that you can grow emotionally as well as intellectually and physically. There is the "actual you" and

91

the "ideal you". The actual you is who you have allowed yourself to become. The ideal you will become more intentional and a better person over time. Remember, when you receive a base salary, you are not being paid for the "actual you," but for the "ideal you."

- Every short-term behavior has long-term consequences. So, if you have chosen to stop growing your interpersonal skills, it will have an impact on the rest of your life for the rest of your life.

- Although it is now possible to do an MRI of our emotional maturity, some people we work with do not want to know their results. They are sometimes concerned that they will be expected to adapt or evolve once they are aware. What good is it to have the freedom to grow if you do not use it?

When someone says that every flower blooms in its own time, it means that the way and speed at which one person learns is likely to be different from the way and speed another person does. What we call learning disabilities are often learning differences. We come from 100% unique material. What would life be like if we all got 1% better every month, 1% better at being a son, aunt, teacher, leader, brother, friend, mother, cousin, father, neighbor, or colleague?

Over 86% of personal issues come from the lack of interpersonal skills to handle them*. No one is looking for perfection. We are only looking for each of us to get a little better as we stumble the mumble on our way to walking the talk.

*https://pumble.com/learn/communication/communication-statistics/

The World Business Forum regularly projects the skills that will be needed for success in the coming years. For 2027, they predict that emotional intelligence will be #11 on the list and most of the others are dependent on emotional literacy.

Here are their projections:

Businesses' top 10 skill priorities for 2027

WORLD ECONOMIC FORUM

1. Analytical thinking
2. Creative thinking
3. AI and big data
4. Leadership and social influence
5. Resilience, flexibility and agility
6. Curiosity and lifelong learning
7. Technological literacy
8. Design and user experience
9. Motivation and self-awareness
10. Empathy and active listening

Type of skill

Cognitive skills   Self-efficacy   Technology skills   Working with others

Source
World Economic Forum, Future of Jobs Report 2023

Note
The skills which organizations will prioritize in workforce development initiatives from 2023 to 2027

If you take a close look at the Top 10 chart above, you'll notice that:

- #5, 6, and 9 are direct outcomes of individual emotional development.

- #4 and 10 are direct outcomes of emotional development as it impacts relationships

- #1 and 2 are only possible with the development of emotions that support thinking in those ways.

- The remainder are listed as 'technology skills' but depend on a worker's *curiosity, ambition, and empathy*, all of which are emotions.

In short, all of the top skills people need now and will need in the future have a close relationship with emotional literacy.

Knowing this, some of us will evolve towards EQ out of inspiration, and some will seek it out due to desperation. Which are you?

I'm at the end of my career. Is this really something I need?

The case has been made for anyone beginning in the profession or mid-career, but why would you need to learn about emotions if you are close to retirement? The short answer is that the day after you retire, you'll still have emotions. A different mix, a different range, a different intensity, but they'll be there with you every moment of every day.

You've probably prepared for retirement by making a financial plan. Maybe there are things you've set aside during your career that you want to spend more time on when it is available. Those are great preparations, but we are asking if you have prepared yourself emotionally.

What can you do today that gives you the best chance to relate to others emotionally when you are no longer on the force? What does it take for you to be emotionally prepared to be with yourself? At work, your purpose may have been big enough to keep your emotions at bay. Now, they will be front and center without the distraction of busyness.

What are some challenging emotions you can expect to show up when you leave the agency?

- Boredom - Nothing interests you.
- Resentment - If you believe there are elements of unfairness in any aspect of your retirement or the way it occurred.
- Disappointment - If you hoped or expected retirement to be better than it is turning out.
- Anxiety - This could be about your health, finances, or could be coming from an unknown source. With more time to reflect, it may be more prevalent.
- Loneliness - You'll likely have more time with yourself and may yearn for more interaction with others.

94

And what about the emotions you are hoping for? These are generally not as difficult to navigate but can sometimes still feel awkward or uncomfortable.

- Pride - You served well and did good.
- Tranquility - Life is calm, quiet, and restful.
- Satisfaction - You have enough, you did enough, you are enough.
- Joy - You can play more or celebrate new things in new ways.
- Excitement - A trip, a new hobby, new relationships, new possibilities;

Any of these and more might show up because of the way your life unfolds. The question we'd ask is, which of the many emotions available will you choose, cultivate, and practice? That aspect of retirement will be up to you as much as your finances.

This is a 'gradually, then suddenly' moment. You'll realize how much structure work gave you. That structure often helps us feel safe and relevant even when we resist it. Your job of understanding and choosing the emotions that support you will be more relevant than ever. So, yes, this is really something you need to begin now.

What can you do now?

Emotional Intelligence (EI)

- You can recognize your own emotions. Your igniters + Your environment = Your personality. Being able to recognize your emotions and what ignites them is a very good step #1.
- You can recognize emotions in others without judgment. Understanding their emotions helps you see how they view their situation and what they need. Their emotions are like a barometer.
- Try to match emotions to the situation. Once I recognize my emotions and the other person's, I can decide to dial up or dial

back my emotions to meet the other person where they need to be met. That is called emotional agility and results in more effective conversations and relationships.

- You can make smart, right, healthy, and successful decisions by combining reason and emotions. As we become more emotions-driven, let's ensure reason remains in the picture. The suggestion is not that you replace intellect with emotions, but simply begin to see them as healthy collaborators.
- You can help others with their emotions. This is where leadership begins with people. First, you must take care of yourself, and then you can take care of others, in the same way firefighters must take care of themselves before they can take care of others.

Mindfulness

Mindfulness is like a rest note in music. Mindfulness means: the appropriate response. What we are focused on is wellness-mindfulness.

If you take the beginning few words from each bullet below, you will have a good definition of emotional maturity/mindfulness that is attributed to Jon Kabat-Zinn, Professor of Medicine Emeritus at the University of Massachusetts Medical School: *Paying attention, on purpose, in the current moment, non-judgmentally.*

- **Pay attention:** Attention leads to awareness, which is the source of choice.
- **On purpose:** our role in a conversation is to enrich, not reduce. For us to enrich conversations, we must bring the best of our intentions and behaviors to the task.
- **In the current moment:** all relationships are built on dialog, and dialog must be treated as important. Respect is the emotion that naturally allows us to acknowledge the value we see in something or someone.

- **Non-judgmentally:** The ability to suspend skepticism and delay judgment takes skill and practice.

Although commentators use different terms to describe the coming caring, sharing, collaborative, or emotional economy, there appears to be significant agreement on two things:

1. The thinking (knowledge) economy has passed its use-by date. A feeling economy that is based on people and relationships is here.

2. Emotions will not replace knowledge. Everyone thought the original microwave would replace the oven. Now kitchens everywhere have both. We need both IQ and EQ, linguistic and emotional literacy, when it comes to making decisions, problem-solving, and building relationships.

Questions to ask yourself

- What emotion(s) are barriers to your emotional learning?
- What emotion(s) would serve you better?
- What emotion(s) are at the root of lifelong learning for you?

- Based on what you read, when you hear other first responders call emotions "touchy-feely," how would you reply now?
- How often do you think about what you think about? Are you an observer or a victim of your thoughts?

Practical application

- **Find a Quiet Space**: Before or after your shift, or during a break, find a quiet spot. This could be in your patrol car, a quiet room at the station, or any other peaceful place within your agency.
- **Adopt a Comfortable Posture**: Sit in a relaxed but upright posture. If in your patrol car, make sure it's parked safely. Place both feet flat on the ground and rest your hands in your lap.
- **Focus on Your Breath**: Close your eyes and bring your attention to your breathing. Notice the sensation of air entering and leaving your nostrils or the rise and fall of your chest or abdomen.
- **Be Present**: As you focus on your breath, your mind might wander. That's okay. Gently bring your attention back to your breathing each time you notice your mind drifting.
- **Expand Your Awareness**: After focusing on your breath for a few minutes, expand your awareness to the sensations in your body. Notice any tension, warmth, or other sensations. Do this without judging or trying to change anything.
- **Observe Non-judgmentally**: Throughout the practice, thoughts, feelings, or sensations will arise. Rather than judging them or getting caught up in them, simply observe them as they come and go. For instance, if you recall a challenging situation from your shift, simply note it as a "memory" and bring your attention back to your breath.
- **Practice Regularly**: Like any skill, mindfulness improves with regular practice. Even just a few minutes a day can make a difference.

- **Apply Mindfulness On Duty**: Over time, you can begin to apply mindfulness during your shifts. For example, if you're in a high-stress situation, take a moment to breathe deeply and ground yourself before reacting. This can help improve decision-making and response times.
- **Join a Group or Find a Teacher**: Many police departments offer mindfulness training for first responders, recognizing its benefits for stress reduction and performance enhancement. Consider joining such a program or seeking external resources.
- **Stay Updated**: As you continue your mindfulness journey, regularly check for new techniques, research, or resources that might be beneficial specifically for first responders.

Remember, mindfulness is about being present and nonjudgmental. It's not about clearing your mind or achieving a particular state. By practicing mindfulness regularly, you can develop greater resilience, improved focus, and better emotional regulation, all of which are crucial for the demanding job of a first responder.

Chapter 9
Imposter Syndrome: Alive and Well in Policing

"The most powerful offer you can make is the genuine you."

Chapter bullets

- You're not alone. Imposter syndrome does not discriminate based on rank, title, intellect, or accomplishments.
- Believing you are 'not enough' or inadequate is simply that - a belief, not the truth.
- It is no more difficult to believe you have worth than that you don't. It is a belief you can choose to change.

Story

As a 14-year police officer, I decided I wanted to become a motorcycle officer. After a rigorous "motor school" and thorough selection process, I was transferred into the Traffic Unit. On my first day of riding alone, quite frankly mainly focusing on keeping the shiny side of the motorcycle up, I received a call from dispatch that a patrol officer was requesting a traffic officer to help on an accident scene.

As I arrived and proudly dismounted my police motorcycle wearing my shiny new motorcycle boots, I approached the veteran patrol officer who explained his dilemma in determining who was at fault in this complex traffic collision. As he was speaking with me, I realized that since it was my first day on the job as a traffic investigator, I still had basically the same knowledge as this patrol officer, because I lacked practical experience. Instead of admitting to the officer, I had no clue on how to answer his question, I simply offered to work the accident for him to save myself from embarrassment. I relieved him from the scene, gathered the pertinent information, and returned to the station to ask a senior traffic officer for assistance.

In the above incident, I lacked the confidence to admit to the patrol officer that I did not know the answer to his question and took on the extra work of completing the investigation myself to publicly "show my worth" and privately save myself from humiliation. When, in fact, the patrol officer would have completely understood if I would have had the humility to admit to him it was my first day, and we probably would have enjoyed a memorable laugh together.

Later in my career, and over a seven-month period, I was quickly promoted from the police officer rank to an Assistant Chief of Police in a large department. My first day on the job as an assistant chief, my assistant placed a stack of paperwork in my inbox. As I went through the documents, I realized that I was not familiar with them as panic and self-doubt set in – I'm not ready for this. Why am I here? I'm not worthy. I immediately gathered up the paperwork, went across the hall, and explained my dilemma to my chief. After he quit laughing, he said, "I can easily teach you how to complete paperwork, but I can't teach you great leadership, which is why I promoted you".

As I would move on to become a Chief of Police myself and later become a City Manager with very little previous city management experience, I would recall my Chief's grace and dignity in how he worked with me to learn budgeting and the administrative tasks while constantly seeking my opinion and valuing my leadership abilities. As a new chief or new city manager in a room full of experienced chiefs or city managers, at times I would still feel self-doubt and that I was somehow not worthy or smart enough to be in the room. When these feelings of a lack of self-confidence would creep into my thoughts, I would remember my mentor's words and remind myself that everyone brings something to the table as a leader and that everyone is a leader regardless of rank.

This chapter helps us understand that when we see ourselves as not worthy of performing a role or being in a new position, in lieu of "faking it until we make it", we must have the emotional awareness to trust our abilities and have confidence that we add value regardless of the position or tenure we hold. In policing, our focus should always be to treat those we serve with respect and dignity. To do so, we must first possess the emotional acumen to treat ourselves with dignity and respect and understand we are worthy, regardless of our background or path, as everyone uniquely adds value.

Steve D., City Manager/Former Police Chief

Some police chiefs share that when they are around other police chiefs, they do not feel like they fit in or are not worthy of being in the same group. Some people repeatedly say they are sorry when they've done nothing that warrants an apology. There are times we compare ourselves to others and come up short because everyone else seems smarter, more successful, and better-liked. We have many clients who have had difficulty stating what they believe or who find it hard to take a stand for themselves. They often tell us they get overlooked or taken advantage of by others.

The term *imposter phenomenon* was first used in an article published in 1978, titled "The Impostor Phenomenon in High Achieving Women: Dynamics and Therapeutic Intervention" by Pauline R. Clance and Suzanne A. Imes. Since then we've come to call a wide collection of experience, including the examples in the first paragraph, *imposter syndrome.*

Sometimes people talk about having low self-esteem, low self-regard, or simply feeling like they are "not enough". They say they fear being "found out" or that they are "unworthy". When one has this way of seeing oneself, it is an incredible barrier.

How can you identify imposter syndrome?

Here are examples of thinking, feelings, or behaviors that fall into the bucket we call imposter syndrome:

- Deep self-doubt
- Constant self-criticism
- Feelings of inadequacy
- Frequent comparison to others
- Anxiety about being 'found out'
- Distrusting your intuition and capabilities
- Believing others have more value than you
- Taking on extra work to prove your worth
- Inability to accept positive assessments or compliments
- Inability to express pride in your achievements
- Defensiveness when challenged

If you feel some or all of these, you are not alone. It is estimated that 80% of us feel a sense of being a fraud or not as important as other people at times. These beliefs often last for years and sometimes never leave us.

What is it?

Although it sounds as if it might be a psychological diagnosis, imposter syndrome is not an illness or disease. It is an experience many of us have, but it is not a mental disorder. Imposter syndrome is not recognized in the **DSM: The Diagnostic and Statistical Manual of Mental Disorders,** the handbook used by healthcare professionals in the United States and much of the world as the authoritative guide to the diagnosis of mental disorders, nor is it listed in the **ICD: The International Classification of Diseases** published by the World Health Organization.

Imposter syndrome is a way of thinking about ourselves that has developed because of things we've heard and interpretations we've made of experiences in our lives. For instance:

- We were one of several children, and we believed that we were not valued as much as our siblings. Sometimes we have evidence, sometimes not.
- As a child, we were told, shown, or came to believe that we were unwanted and thus not valued or valuable.
- We were born into a group or culture that was treated as secondary. The group might have been based on gender, culture, religion, ethnicity, or other aspects of us that were not our choice.
- We had individual characteristics that other people didn't value or ridiculed, such as being outside of the norm for height, weight, color, speed of action, accent, appearance, or a wide range of other traits.
- We were told by someone we looked up to that we would never succeed or that we were worthless.

Or perhaps we had a wonderful and cheerful childhood but still came to see ourselves as less capable and less important than others.

If you step back and take an evidence-based look at yourself, you may find that there isn't much to support the belief you are inadequate as a human being, so perhaps you do have equal worth.

What is the benefit; what is the cost?

Although people who view themselves as inadequate often suffer as a result, the impact isn't always negative. It can fuel them to work harder in an effort to prove their worth. It can help them achieve things they might not otherwise. Self-doubt can drive them to get multiple degrees, strive for the pinnacle of their profession, or excel at sports.

104

And then there is the suffering.

The costs of seeing yourself as less valuable than others can lead to despair, self-doubt, and a sense that you don't belong. You might believe others do not want to be associated with you and feel excluded. Besides the lack of self-acceptance and appreciation, the biggest cost most people experience from imposter syndrome is a nagging sense they will be found out and shunned or at least lose whatever success they've achieved. That preoccupation shadows every thought, word, and action. Suffering is pain with meaning, and when one constantly associates suffering with a feeling of unworthiness, it can be a self-perpetuating cycle that hinders the realization of one's true value and potential.

What can you do about it?

The most common advice we're given is to "fake it until we make it". In other words, act as if you are valuable until you believe it. That isn't a bad suggestion, even if vague on how it should be implemented, but it isn't sufficient to effect the change.

The authors have proposed that emotions are the energy that moves us and that they underlie all our behaviors. If you want to move beyond imposter syndrome and achieve an absolute belief in your self-worth, you need to cultivate a new emotion, intervene in your thinking, and modify your posture.

The emotion that generates the belief we have value is *dignity*. In dignity, you believe, without question, that you are as valuable as every other human being. That allows you to take a stand for yourself. You do not need permission or approval to believe what you believe or to feel what you feel. You are whole and deserving of respect and self-respect. You decide what is best for you and take responsibility for the consequences.

Your thinking and self-talk are supportive. You do not belittle yourself. You are honest and without pretense. You regularly have thoughts like "I am enough", "I am worthy", "I decide for me", or "I'm valuable just the way I am".

The posture or disposition of dignity is visible in many characters. Archetypically, it is the emotion and posture of a monarch; a king or queen. You can envision their erect posture, steady gaze, and calm demeanor. They look to the horizon or future and walk with steady confidence. Their posture projects strength and self-assurance. When we feel dignity, we extend dignity to others. It is impossible not to and remain in dignity.

But, one does not need to be a king or queen in a literal sense. Dignity can be accessed by people of every variety - truck drivers, actors, chefs, soccer players, rich, poor, educated, illiterate, successful, and not successful alike. Police as well. It is available to all humans. The question is whether we are aware of its power and potential. And whether we've committed to developing it.

The messages that you are inadequate are not going to stop. People will continue, intentionally or not, to demean one another, and if you do not have a filter, you will not be able to maintain a belief in your adequacy and legitimacy. If you long for the belief that you are of value just as you are, dignity is the path. Add these elements to "fake it until you make it", and you will get there.

Questions to ask yourself

- What phrases do you think about yourself most often? Are they self-critical or self-affirming?
- Where did you learn to think about yourself in the way you do?
- Does it elevate dignity or undermine it?
- Which of the other characteristics listed above describe you?

Practical application

Remember when your elementary teacher or mother or aunt told you to "sit up straight"? They didn't say that just because they thought your posture was poor. They may not have known how to guide you through shaping your whole body to support the emotion of dignity, but they were pushing you in the right direction.

Like all emotions, there are two elements required to generate dignity: Your thoughts and your body.

- Thoughts that generate dignity: "I am enough", "I'm ok just as I am", "I decide for me", "I am worthy", and many others. You need to find the words that inspire and feel right to you. Start searching.
- The body that supports dignity:
  - Feet flat on the floor or ground when sitting or standing.
  - Walking with a measured pace and always one foot fully planted.
  - Spine erect and elongated.
  - Shoulders rolled back so they run straight across your chest.
  - Neck straight.
  - Head balanced. Not tipped forward nor back, or to the side.

- ○ Eyes softly focused on the horizon.
- ○ Face relaxed; not smiling or serious. Think "Mona Lisa."
- ○ Breath even and moderately deep.

Practice embodying dignity twice each day for 5 minutes. Assume the posture and repeat the phrase you chose. It may feel awkward, uncomfortable, or silly. It is probably new, so of course it does. Just do it. Every day for a week. Check what has changed. The answers the authors hear most often are "bigger, stronger, more self-assured, more confident, clearer, more peaceful, and happier". Not bad for an investment of 70 minutes.

Do it for another two weeks. Check what has changed. Send us an email. We'd love to know.

Chapter 10
Emotional Literacy is not Something you Believe in, it is Something you do.

"Between the stimulus and response, there is a space. And in that space lies our freedom and power to choose our response. In our response lies our growth and our freedom."

- Viktor Frankl

Chapter bullets

- Today, you will eat, sleep, and experience emotions. The degree to which you pay attention to the way you do those things will make all the difference.
- As one emotion is challenging you there are 200 other emotions you can choose from that might serve you better.
- You get to decide the emotion in which you are going to live your experience.

Story

When I was first promoted to supervisor, I was inexperienced; I lacked formal and informal training. Yet, I believed that when my officers came in to ask a question, discuss a personal matter, voice a concern, or challenge my direction, I was to know the answer, the solution, and have an immediate response, as if the moment I was promoted instantly instilled in me the key to the supervisory vault. I was responsible for solving whatever it was…… right then and there. I was emotionally illiterate.

Looking back, I recognized myself, on several occasions, developing an immediate response in mid-conversation, and from that point on, until I was able to provide my response to the officer, I was no longer paying attention to what they were saying. I was waiting for the pause in the conversation to provide my great wisdom or to give my justified view. This internal urge to respond immediately somehow was connected to my effectiveness as a supervisor. I had the answers. I wasn't going to be challenged and not have an appropriate and immediate response, regardless of the emotion that planted the response.

Fast forward to the promotional process for Assistant Chief, my first opportunity to participate in the process. One stage of the process was to be interviewed by department directors within the city who the police department works with most frequently. I entered the Fire Chief's office for my first interview. As I looked around his office, I saw a sign above his door visible to him as he sat behind his desk, "Shut up and Listen." The resulting conversation with that Fire Chief will remain with me for the rest of my life.

It emphasized the point that not everyone is looking for me to solve their problems. Employees, at times, simply need to be heard, to vent. Truly listening is providing a safe and confidential place others can trust. I also realized this applies throughout my life, not only in my professional world.

For those conversations that required a response, I learned that if I'm truly listening, I'm not formulating a response in my mind as my emotions build and sway while the other person is speaking. If I'm truly listening, it feels natural to temporarily pause when they are done before I respond. This safeguards against a potentially emotionally charged knee-jerk response I would regret and allows me an opportunity to develop a thoughtful response.

Since this pivotal moment in my career, it has been an ongoing goal to continue to improve and build my emotional literacy. I am not perfect, and I can assure you, my road has not been without its potholes. However, I am self-aware and am purposely striving to model emotional literacy the best I can while encouraging others to be aware and start their journey in building their emotional literacy.

Brad F., Chief of Police

Reaction vs Response

Every emotion dictates a reaction. With practice, we can modify our reactions, but we cannot eliminate them. Nor would we want to. Ducking your head when startled can help you avoid injury. Greeting a friend with a spontaneous smile confirms your affection for them.

Reactions, however, do not always get us what we want or need. For that, we need another emotional skill, which is *crafting a response*. Imagine you feel envy because someone got a promotion you wanted. Your reaction might be to try to undermine that person's success. That is rarely productive.

The response your envy is trying to point you towards might be to better understand what you need to do to be the next person promoted. You could ask yourself if you are making unwarranted assumptions about being ready. Perhaps a sincere conversation with the appropriate people to let them know about your interest and preparation would be more helpful than stewing in envy.

Reactions are automatic and occur before we have time to think. We could illustrate the dynamic as an hourglass with emotions passing through bit by bit to thoughts:

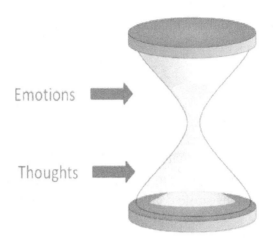

A response could be illustrated as the reverse: thoughts flowing through to emotions:

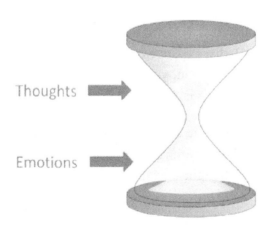

Both reactions and responses are useful and even essential, but the competence many of us have not developed well is the latter. Navigating from reaction to response can be slowed or stopped altogether when the neck of the hourglass is obstructed, which is not helpful. In those moments we feel stuck or caught in an emotion and lose our emotional agility.

There are many ways to develop our ability to respond effectively, but it seems that they all are based on creating a momentary time gap for our systems to come back to balance. That moment allows our thinking to re-engage so we remember the huge palette of emotions we can leverage to respond.

We all know the idea of counting to 10 before we say anything. We know we can walk away, not answer the call, or close the computer. But, many of us don't have a method we use habitually. What is yours?

Your emotional palette

If you were to grab a pen and paper and list the emotions that come to mind, how many would you capture? This list is the pallet you paint from when it comes to your emotions. If you can list only 20, then that reflects the breadth and depth of your ability to recognize, name, and express your emotions. If you listed between 15 and 25 you have the typical emotional vocabulary of an educated adult. Nothing to be ashamed of, but so much more is possible.

How do you differentiate between courage and boldness? Can you distinguish the differences between anger, frustration, and resentment? If you do not know, you are experiencing the emotion of confusion, and a confused mind says "no".

There are people who believe self-analysis is the answer. They think they know exactly why they do the things they do: A tyrannical mother, an abusive husband, the poverty they were raised in, or a childhood of indulgence and privilege. Those are not the source of their behavior, they are excuses for it. Insight is cheap, but of limited value.

113

These people have insight, but instead of using it as a means to develop new and hopefully more helpful behavior, they use it as a reason to continue with old, destructive behavior. They believe they are victims. The list of people who have done them wrong is long. They are not willing to go through the pain it takes to change, even though the pain of staying the same is killing them.

Building emotional literacy

Do you remember how you learned to read? First, you probably noticed other people looking at marks in a book that were meaningless to you. Someone may have shown you their value as words, or you may have figured it out by watching. Little by little you noticed that the words were made up of letters arranged in a specific way. You related those words to the sounds people made when they spoke them aloud. And from there, you progressed to reading and eventually writing. By these steps, you became linguistically literate.

A similar process works with emotions, but instead of focusing on written words, you notice your feelings and their relationship to stories and impulses. The steps are not so different:

- First, you notice what you are feeling, which alerts you to an emotion
- Then, you try to name the emotion as accurately as you can
- From there, you build your knowledge and understanding
- Finally, you put all of this to work for you

Imagined as steps, it looks like this:

Steps to build emotional literacy

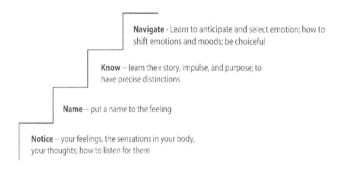

Navigate - Learn to anticipate and select emotion; how to shift emotions and moods; be choiceful

Know – learn their story, impulse, and purpose; to have precise distinctions

Name – put a name to the feeling

Notice – your feelings, the sensations in your body, your thoughts; how to listen for them

Steps

1. **Pause and notice your energy:** High or low? Forward or backward? Moving or still? What are you thinking, telling yourself, or believing at this moment? What is your impulse? What do you feel like doing?

It sounds simple to 'pause and notice' but we live active lives, always busy, always on the move. How can you incorporate 'moments of noticing' into your day?

2. **Name your emotion**: Again, it sounds simple enough, but most people find it quite difficult. We feel and act but don't stop to identify which emotion is driving our actions.

Research shows that naming our emotions is a key step in emotional regulation or choosing the emotion that will serve the moment best.

3. **Build your knowledge**: What information is each emotion offering? What is the impulse we feel in each? What is its

purpose? How do we know if what we are feeling is anger or resentment? What differentiates a mood from an emotion? Why is that important?

You've spent most of your life gaining knowledge and honing skills and close to zero time building emotional understanding. It isn't just you, none of us has. Now is the time.

4. **Learn to navigate emotionally:** Plan future conversations or interactions. Shift emotions that are barriers. Forget about controlling your emotions. Learn to dance with them, befriend them, and trust them to inform and guide you.

Your emotions are a gift every bit as much as your intellect and body. You are incomplete as a human being if you ignore or deny them. Embracing them makes you whole.

And repeat, and repeat, and repeat until emotions become habitual and transparent considerations in all aspects of your life. You've arrived!

Questions to ask yourself

- Have you created a safe and supportive environment where colleagues and reports feel comfortable exploring, expressing, and reflecting upon their emotions without judgment?
- Are you modeling emotional literacy in your behavior and demonstrating the self-awareness and regulation that you are looking for in others?
- How aware are you of your own self-awareness gap? Self-scouting is always good to do.
- How are you staying updated with the latest research, tools, and techniques in emotional literacy, and how frequently are you reassessing your methods to ensure they are effective and relevant for your agency?

Practical application

Emotion-Centered Professional Development Working Sessions:

- Integrate comprehensive learning modules that focus on noticing, naming, and navigating emotions.
- Use practical scenarios and interactive sessions to simulate challenges first responders might face at home, at work, and when stressed. This helps in understanding the complexity of human emotions and promotes better decision-making, problem-solving, and relationship-building during intense situations.

Mindfulness and Resilience Practices

- Introduce regular mindfulness exercises, meditation, and resilience-building practices. These techniques can enhance self-awareness, stress relief, and improve emotional regulation. Over time, first responders can develop the ability to remain calm, focused, and compassionate, even under pressure.

Chapter 11
Successive Approximation

"When in doubt, just take the next small step"

- Paul Coelho

Chapter bullets

- How do you eat an elephant? One bite at a time
- True knowing is visible in our actions
- Everyone can be my teacher

Story

Elevated positions in police leadership, such as deputy chief, are just that.....they are elevated. This truly means you see things you didn't see before as a result of the higher altitude. While achieving the rank is commendable, it comes with a complete set of challenges unique to the title. However, probably the single largest challenge of all is figuring out who you are supposed to be now that you occupy the position. I remember how the more than twenty-five years of prior experience I had in multiple different ranks and responsibilities just seemed to vanish after being promoted to deputy chief. I felt like I knew absolutely nothing, and there was no way I was the person who should be in the position.

The truth was right there in front of me all along. I just had to step back and realize all of my past experiences and all of the ranks that came and went with them had not gone anywhere. They had all helped lead me to right where I was supposed to be. But back to the earlier question...who was I now? It turns out the answer was not as big of a secret as I originally thought it was. I was still very much me. Although my rank changed, I did not. I cannot overstate how important that simple, yet elusive reality is. It was the exact same formula that worked so well in every other rank I had ever been blessed with.

You are still you, and this being true is one of the overwhelming reasons you now hold that rank in the first place. Understanding how self-awareness and emotional intelligence play a part in your continued success is the hallmark of true leadership. Recognizing the role you play has grown exponentially regarding how you act, treat others, and face each challenge laid before you. This is of equal importance at work and at home. It has been said true leaders stand apart, they do not stand alone.

This means we cannot do it by ourselves. In addition to being a leader, we are also to be facilitators, teachers, and, yes, at times, even the student. I had to admit my rank did not make me all-knowing or how important the need was to foster relationships with everyone who worked with me. Being aware of the stifling effects of a closed and defensive mindset when I would find myself out of my "knowledge comfort zone" has kept me centered and connected with the very people I need the most. Accept we all have limitations, know yours, and stay open to learning every day.

Leave the defensive mindset at the door and focus on being a positive, motivating presence for everyone around you. Elevated positions also mean we can elevate everyone else right along with us toward the achievement of great things. I want to leave you with a phrase I heard a long time ago which still resonates with me today. "God does not just call the equipped, He also equips the called". Regardless of your faith or beliefs, never forget what you've been called and equipped to do. Be the leader you would want to follow and look for every opportunity to be the best you can be for everyone, including yourself.

Timothy V., Deputy Chief

Successive Approximation Individually Applied

When the rhythm changes, so must our dance. Learning to do that sometimes happens in one gigantic leap. At times, it is a delightful experience, and other times, a painful and jarring one. But when you choose to learn, it generally happens through successive approximation, getting a little better each day. This happens when we are focused on and working towards a new way of being.

One small change in perception can create a big change in our view of the future. Becoming a better son, aunt, husband, cousin, neighbor, or colleague happens in tiny steps over time. But simply time passing does make you better. Effective learning requires intentionality. Where can you start?

Mindset

Mindset, sometimes referred to as mental attitude or beliefs, is the #1 predictor of success when it comes to your emotional literacy journey:

- **Self-Protection Mindset:** A defensive stance in which you stop being curious or appreciative and spend your energy resisting what is unfamiliar.
- **Connection Mindset:** To be open, present and immersed in the moment, able to respond from curiosity, appreciation, and gratitude.

Disruption is a change to something we were certain of. When you experience disruption, you can either move into self-protection mode or connection mode. Your choice.

In our attention economy, everything competes with everything else. This makes our attention a commodity that everyone is fighting for. Attention is your currency. You trade it for things you believe are of value.

And, you cannot multitask when it comes to complex activities. One of the great myths of our time is that it is possible to effectively work on two things at the same time. This is the false application of a principle in the way computers operate to humans. We work differently. What we can do is shift our attention from one thing to another very quickly, so we can expect that people working in an attention economy are distracted much of the time. Most people we teach love learning; it is the paying attention part that is difficult.

Emotional regulation

You regulate all sorts of things every day. The temperature in your house or car, the amount you eat, what you do or don't say, the pace at which you walk. Regulation is our tool for moving from discomfort to comfort or being more effective. Why wouldn't you leverage regulation with your emotions?

At times, a little more ambition would energize you to finish some paperwork. Other times, a little less would allow you to rest. Increasing curiosity helps you continue searching for an answer, but sometimes, it just annoys other people. Deep resentment can drive you to acts of vengeance, but when it is weak or lacking, you lose track of what you believe is fair treatment.

Emotions are fluid. They come and they go, they rise and they fall. Regulation allows you to choose what level of an emotion will serve you best in the moment. And it is a competence we can all learn. We've lived for a long time with the myth that our emotions control us, but there's another side to the coin.

In the table that follows, you'll find suggestions about how to dial up or dial down ten emotions, although the concept extends to all emotions.

Emotion	Definition	To dial up/strengthen	To dial down/diminish
Anger	The belief that something unjust has been done to me or someone I care about.	**Step 1.** Ask yourself if there is an emotion blocking anger for you. Common ones are fear, embarrassment, shame, or guilt. **Step 2.** Consider whether it serves you to avoid anger or if there is a negative consequence. **Step 3.** Find a situation in which beginning to express anger is safe. For instance, improvisational theater allows participants to experiment with emotions outside their typical range.	**Step 1.** Naming anger changes it, so the first step is to acknowledge that we are feeling anger. **Step 2.** Change your breathing pattern. In anger, our breath is rapid and shallow. Slow and deepen your breath. Broaden your focus. In anger, our eyes focus intensely. Relax and broaden your gaze. **Step 3.** Create a pause. Biochemical activity is an element of anger. Pausing allows your limbic system to begin returning to a rest state and for your anger to lessen.
Frustration	The belief that something is taking longer than it should.	**Step 1.** Recognize the value of frustration. Some of us refuse to admit we feel frustration because we think it is morally wrong or we are embarrassed. **Step 2.** Accept that you feel frustrated and connect with the energy of your frustration to become accustomed to it. **Step 3.** Once frustration becomes familiar, practice ways to channel it into actions that will speed things up.	**Step 1.** Recognize the value of frustration. It isn't to punish the other person but to try to get things aligned with your expectations. **Step 2.** Check your standards or expectations. Are they realistic for the situation and person involved? If not, reset your expectations. **Step 3.** If you believe your standards are realistic, turn frustration into curiosity by exploring "Why is this taking so long:" or "How could this be speeded up?"
Compassion	To be present with another person for the	**Step 1.** Center yourself and put your attention on the other person.	**Step 1.** Ask yourself what problem is being created by too much compassion.

Emotion	Definition	To dial up/strengthen	To dial down/diminish
	sake of understanding	**Step 2.** Acknowledge to them that their experience is legitimate and that there is nothing wrong with them. **Step 3.** Remain present.	**Step 2.** Imagine or search the list at the back of the book for an emotion that would be more appropriate. **Step 3.** Identify the narrative of that story, and whenever you feel pulled into compassion, intervene in your thinking.
Curiosity	The desire to know more because we believe it may be of value	**Step 1:** Put your attention on the subject or person you'd like to be more curious about. **Step 2:** Ask yourself how listening to them or investigating the topic could be beneficial to you **Step 3:** Allow yourself to voice the questions that come to you.	**Step 1:** Ask yourself if what you are feeling is curiosity or the discomfort of not knowing. **Step 2:** Ask yourself if knowing the answer will bring you more peace or if you are looking for control. **Step 3:** Search for an emotion, such as faith or trust, that allows you to feel at peace with not knowing.
Acceptance	To acknowledge that things are as they are regardless of whether we agree with or like them that way	**Step 1:** Identify the desire or expectation you have that keeps you from accepting things as they are. **Step 2:** Acknowledge that the world doesn't care if you like the way things are, but they are still that way. **Step 3:** Practice declaring that things are as they are and that it is not within your power to change them.	**Step 1:** Check that what you are feeling is acceptance and not resignation. **Step 2:** Even as you accept the way things are, ask yourself if there is a way you would like them to change. **Step 3:** Notice what emotions emerge - excitement, yearning, ambition - and begin to focus on those.

Emotion	Definition	To dial up/strengthen	To dial down/diminish
Resentment	To believe that we or someone we care about has been treated unfairly	**Step 1:** Think about situations you've experienced in which you feel you did not get what was due you. **Step 2:** Notice the story of unfairness that emerges. **Step 3:** Articulate for yourself what you would ask for that removes the unfairness. If appropriate, make the request.	**Step 1:** Ask yourself what is unfair about the situation. **Step 2:** Acknowledge that your resentment is based on the belief you did not get what you deserve or were treated unfairly, and that is subjective. **Step 3:** Either make a request that resolves the unfairness as you see it, OR accept that it will always look unfair to you.
Tolerance	To endure a situation believing it will eventually change	**Step 1:** Identify the situation or person that is irritating you. **Step 2:** Ask yourself how long the situation is likely to last **Step 3:** Declare that the best way for you to live through the situation is to endure it until it changes.	**Step 1:** Ask yourself what you want to stop tolerating. **Step 2:** Explore why you tolerate it - a sense of obligation? Fear? Guilt? **Step 3:** Decide what emotion can help you step out of tolerating - Boldness? Dignity? Frustration? - and work towards that.
Loyalty	To defend a group to which we belong	**Step 1:** Think about the importance of the group to your life. **Step 2:** Ask yourself why you don't speak up on behalf of the group and whether embarrassment or shame might be barriers. **Step 3:** Begin taking small steps to support and share the value of the group to you.	**Step 1:** Clarify for yourself where your loyalty lies - with your team? With your leader? With yourself? **Step 2:** Ask yourself if the strength of your loyalty is balanced and appropriate or if it may be blinding you to something important. **Step 3:** Rebalance your loyalties to include all parties.

Emotion	Definition	To dial up/strengthen	To dial down/diminish
Dignity	To believe we are worthy and equal in value to all other human beings	**Step 1:** Ask yourself where you learned that you were not of value. **Step 2:** Consider the source of that learning **Step 3:** Begin a program of strengthening your belief that you are a legitimate human being of equal value to all other human beings.	**In the authors' view, it is not possible to have too much dignity. Since dignity is not comparative, it will not cause us to believe we are more important than others. A unique aspect of dignity is that when we act from dignity, we extend dignity to others.**
Courage	The ability to act despite feeling fear	**Step 1:** Name the fear that is provoking the need for courage. **Step 2:** Ask yourself if avoiding the fear or confronting it will be more productive. **Step 3:** Acting from your heartfelt belief, step into action.	**Step 1:** Recognize the possible consequences of acting in a dangerous situation. **Step 2:** Ask yourself if there is an alternate way to approach the situation. **Step 3:** Explore other emotions such as prudence, patience, or tolerance.

Emotional navigation

Why navigation rather than control? The short answer is that no human controls their emotions. The longer answer is that, if we could, it wouldn't be as helpful as we imagine.

If we could switch emotions on and off, we would most likely increase the ones that feel pleasant and decrease the uncomfortable ones. But, as we've written, comfort and discomfort are simply the mechanisms an emotion has available to get our attention. We need the reaction that comes with emotions such as anger, envy, and disappointment just as much as we need the reaction we feel in love, joy, and exhilaration.

Once we've reacted and recognized the emotion we feel, we are faced with a choice. Now what? Will I stay in the emotion that was ignited, or would it be more useful to shift to another emotion? That is one type of emotional navigation. I'm here, and I want to move there. I feel disappointment and believe acceptance would be more useful. I feel affection but believe that respect would be more appropriate.

There is a second possibility with emotional navigation, which is planning our future. When faced with a potentially contentious conversation, what emotion gets triggered in you? Perhaps apprehension or anger. Ask yourself whether that emotion will create the conversation you want to have. Is there an emotion that could potentially be of greater value? What about curiosity, compassion, or dignity? Emotional navigation is the tool that lets you prepare emotionally for upcoming situations.

What is the first step?

- Begin with the idea that there are over 200 emotions available to explore. Look at the list in the appendix. How many are familiar? How many have you felt? How many do you recognize and understand?

- Think about getting your emotional house in order. What emotion is a barrier to who you envision yourself to be? What emotion would help you be that person? What emotion would give you what you need, whether it is rest, energy, closer relationships, or time alone?

- Acknowledge that you will never know it all. The world of emotions is as big as the world of reason, intellect, and knowledge. There is always something new and as yet undiscovered.

- Look less for perfection in others and yourself. Emotions exist to allow us to adapt. If you feel guilt, what is it telling you about the misalignment between your values and behavior? If someone treats you in a way you perceive as disrespectful, what emotion might be driving them?

- Change will not take as long as you imagine. Change begins the moment you say to yourself, "I'm not satisfied," followed by the question, "What emotion would help me be the way I would like to be?"

The role of the language you use

Changes in language accompany changes in behavior. Our personalities shift depending on the language we use. Language reveals the observer you are, what you value, and your relationship with others. It also is rooted in emotions. Why did your parents insist you call the neighbor Mr. Roberts rather than Bill? It showed respect. If you say someone is "crazy" vs. "that person lives with bipolar disorder," it reveals more about you than it does about them.

There are phrases and expressions that reveal how first responders see the world. These would be a good place to begin the change.

- "I am old school". Being old school isn't wrong. Being 'old school' sometimes helps protect some needed policies and traditions. But ask yourself if being 'old school' is rooted in respect or stubbornness. When you say you are 'old school,' it lets others know loud and clear that your willingness to change or learn something new is close to zero. Some words count, and some words count more.
- Calling your awesome work colleagues "non-sworn". We are currently digging for water on Mars and there is a job title out there that starts with "non"? Some agencies call their colleagues without guns and arresting power "civilians". Some agencies see these great colleagues as "Professional Staff". Is this just semantics? You decide. You might be saying, "Well we don't actually mean that," and we say, "We

know", and that is why we all need to be more attentive to and intentional with our words.

- We need the chief's "buy-in". Buy-in is such a tricky thing. Buy-in works when we have a budget and what we are being asked to do is convenient. When you got married, signed your mortgage papers, or swore "to protect and serve," no one asked you if you were "bought-in". They asked for your commitment. Buy-in is supportive. Commitment is involvement.

- "Let me be brutally honest". The second I, Marcel, hear you say that to me, I think, "Okay, let's go". Being brutally honest means, I should be able to put on my boxing gloves and hit right back just as hard...'cuz you know...we're just being "brutally honest". You can be honest without being brutal, but today, we are going to leave all of our relational skills on the ground and cut right in.

Emotions to master first

There are a handful of emotions that shape and define your days at work. Learn these first, and you'll have the 20% that makes 80% of the difference.

Equanimity:
Story: "I can see the situation from all sides."
Impulse: To consider in a calm, even-handed manner.
Purpose: Allows us to consider things from a balanced emotional state.

Equanimity allows you to take in many perspectives at once. Its impact on your thinking begins with the realization that what looks like fact and reality to you is not the only possibility. Curiosity is always nearby. Stubbornness and certainty are nowhere to be seen.

Dispassion:

Story: "I choose to set aside my most intense emotions for the moment."
Impulse: To act pragmatically.
Purpose: Lets us focus on getting things done.

Dispassion is an emotion that allows you to set aside emotions and focus on data and procedures. It lets you choose to be emotionally uninvolved in the situation. Not distant, not uncaring, not closed, but focused on the thing that needs to be done. Dispassion allows you to set aside judgment and observe what is.

Staying balanced. Staying present. These are two behaviors your agency needs and needs from you. There is relaxed and ready, and there is rigid and ready. Dispassion and equanimity allow you to be relaxed and ready.

Choosing a response

Let's imagine there is a policy change within your agency. You may experience or encounter...

Frustration: "Why should we have to do this?" Frustration occurs because we have expectations around speed and ease that aren't being met. We often think that frustration means that something is "wrong", when, in fact, it is just informing us that something is not happening in alignment with our standards for how fast or how easily something will happen.

Disappointment: "I was hoping they weren't going to do this". Disappointment tells us that there is a misalignment between what we hope or expect and how life is happening. Expectations come from your imagination about how the future will be. Disappointment is not something others do to you. You have an expectation, the other person behaves in a different manner, you realize there is a gap, and feel the disappointment of things not being as you imagined they would be.

Indifference: "Whatever". It's all the same to you if X or Y happens. It allows you to give up your need to lead or decide and follow what others suggest. It is not necessarily negative or a sign of weakness. In the case of a policy change, you will not resist, but neither will you be its champion. You are willing to walk on either side of the road.

Resignation: "There's nothing I can do about it". You give up. You surrender. You don't even voice your feelings about the change because you believe it wouldn't make any difference.

Resentment: "This is so unfair". You shouldn't have to do this because it puts an undue burden on you. As long as you feel resentment you will look for ways to get even for the unfairness you feel. Could be small things, could be big things, but they will all be efforts to get even.

How could you respond by leveraging emotions?

Tolerance:

Story: "I'll put up with the change."
Impulse: To endure.
Purpose: Allow us to continue with activities we don't enjoy or might not agree with.

Acceptance:

Story: "It is so even though I may not agree, endorse, or like it."
Impulse: To be at peace with what is.
Purpose: Help us align with reality.

Curiosity:

Story: "I wonder why they're making the change?"

Impulse: To seek information often by asking open questions.

Purpose: Helps us see intent, purpose, or value. Generates understanding.

Remember what we shared earlier: you can't boss passion, love, or "want to." As a supervisor, you can only be a 49% shareholder in someone else's success. Even strong verbal arguments will not change another person's emotions. A person's beliefs are rooted in their emotions, and they will continue believing what they believe until their emotion shifts.

One fascinating characteristic of both beliefs and emotions is that we are ready to go to the mat for them even though they are not real. They are just the way we interpret life. And who decides how we interpret life if not us?

Anger

Of the two hundred emotions we share, anger is one of the most talked about. It makes most of us uncomfortable and is feared by many, although some people love the energy it brings. Yet, when asked, many people aren't clear what triggers anger.

Anger is provoked when you feel there has been an injustice done to you or someone you care about. It creates an impulse to stop the injustice and, sometimes, punish the source. It allows you to identify injustice and, by extension, justice. Anger is not inherently violent or aggressive as we sometimes believe and can be expressed quietly yet powerfully by ignoring someone or turning a cold shoulder.

If you recall the last time you felt anger, you will find a link to injustice, something you believed was morally wrong. That is a deep place for an emotion to spring from. Your sense of what is right and wrong, just and unjust. Because of its depth, we feel urgency to stop the injustice we are experiencing or witnessing.

One of the interesting things about anger is that it is only ignited when 'we believe something is unjust'. That means that our anger emerges from our values and beliefs and does not exist independently. Things that anger you do not always anger other people, and vice versa.

Knowing that can help us understand ourselves and keep our anger in perspective. This is more inner work. If anger is one of your go-to emotions or one you avoid at all costs, take a look.

- What judgements do you have about anger as an emotion?
- What experiences generally trigger yours?
- What beliefs or values of yours are being challenged?
- Do you avoid anger even when you witness or experience injustice?
- What emotions keep you from investigating and leveraging your anger to restore justice?

Service vs. Sacrifice

Many people become first responders because, in their souls, they were born to serve and protect. Some officers see themselves as part of "Communities protecting Communities" or even "We are Them".

Serving others feeds our soul. It allows one to move beyond oneself and sometimes be the difference that makes the difference in someone else's life. It nurtures and energizes us.

Sacrifice is depleting. Sacrifice is giving up one thing for another. What you give up is often a part of you. Sacrifice is sometimes noble and what we choose, but it can be unsustainable.

One is not better than the other, but the consequences they carry differ. For a wide variety of reasons, sacrifice is growing as a part of policing. If you joined to serve and now feel you are too often sacrificing your well-being, you might want to work on a mechanism for rebalancing.

Compassion and self-compassion

Be mindful about looking for perfection in others. It may be a reflection of your desire for perfection in you. Look instead for progress. Over the years, we all have evolved in the clothes we wear, the foods we eat, and the friends we choose. Let's also keep evolving in our self-awareness, our social awareness, and our situational awareness through time and over time. If we do, we ensure that the best day we have had on this planet is one that is still out ahead of us.

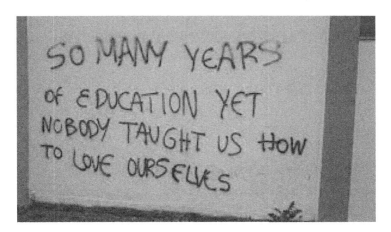

Self-awareness > Ego?

In my work around psychometrics, I am often called in to meet with agencies that have employees exhibiting blind spots. These blind spots cause them to have blind behaviors, which prevent them from doing their best work. After meeting with these employees, I notice that their behavior generally comes down to ego and intention.

Ego and intention are the two ways we win in this world. Everything on this planet has intention. An acorn has intention. If you crack the acorn open, you see the start of a giant oak tree. If I planted the acorn, it would never come out of the ground as a pumpkin plant or an apple tree. Its intention is one hundred percent pure. Just like a dog can sniff fear, humans can tell when someone's intentions are not in alignment with what they say they are.

Self-awareness, social awareness, and situational awareness are all parts of emotional competence. What I am constantly trying to figure out is where ego ends, and self-confidence begins. Self-confidence is a state of non-judgement. Ego kicks in when you start to compare yourself to others. When your ego is bigger than your self-confidence, there is a higher probability you'll lead with your ego. When you are self-aware, you are more likely to lead with intention.

Looking at ego from an emotional perspective

The word ego was chosen by Sigmund Freud's translator for the German word *ich,* or *I,* in English. When we talk about ego, it is often because we believe someone has a 'big ego' or is 'ego-centric'.

The size of your ego depends on your perception of yourself. There are four emotions that are elemental to shaping your way of seeing yourself. They are *humility, pride, arrogance, and hubris.* The table below shows their root, meaning, and how they affect our self-image and behavior.

Emotion	Root	Belief or story	Behavior
Humility	*"Of the earth"*	We are grounded in our view or ourselves	We act without pretension
Pride	*"To congratulation oneself"*	We believe we are or have done something good	We want to share with others who we are or what we've done

Arrogance	*"Assuming, overbearing, insolent"*	We believe we are morally superior or more important than others	We condescend toward others and treat them as inferior
Hubris	*"Presumption toward the gods"*	We believe we are untouchable	We act with impunity

Pay particular attention to the column marked "Behavior". That is where your ego becomes visible. We all have these four emotions in our makeup. The one we live most naturally is seen as our character. People who are accused of having big or oversized egos generally act from either arrogance or hubris, or both. When we look down on others or believe we are untouchable, we separate ourselves from others, which is not conducive to effective relationships.

Humility

You know by now that our understanding of any particular emotion is an interpretation. We believe it means x even though others may see it differently. That is what we would like to propose about humility. It has often been defined as "putting oneself below others", but there are two other emotions that mean that. One is ***servility***, in which we believe our place is to act as a servant for others; someone is our master. The other is ***obsequiousness***, which is the emotion that causes us to grovel or beg in hope of acceptance.

The interpretation of humility we find effective is that it is the emotion in which we own all that we are and claim nothing that we are not. We do not resort to pretense. We are who we are. We have skills and capabilities, and we have shortcomings. We don't hesitate to share our skills and knowledge when appropriate, but we do not overstate them.

Humility is a fantastic balancing emotion. It keeps us living in the reality of who we are, never pretending to be more or less than we can demonstrate. And, like all emotions, the more we practice it, the stronger it gets.

The benefit of living in humility is that it is accompanied by a great deal of peace and self-assurance. We know who we are and who we are not. That allows others to know us more fully, which is, after all, what connection is all about.

So what about vulnerability?

Whenever the authors introduce emotions, the word vulnerability shows up. Curiously, there are mixed views about whether vulnerability is positive or negative. One is that it opens us up to being hurt or mocked. The other is that it allows people to connect with and understand us.

The authors' view is that being unguarded emotionally is neither inherently good or bad, positive or negative. Being unguarded allows certain possibilities and closes others. Being guarded allows different possibilities and can, at times, act as a barrier.

The art of vulnerability is balancing between being "open enough to connect with others" while being "defended enough to protect yourself".

Think about your eyes. If they were always closed, they would be protected, and injury would be unlikely, but you wouldn't be able to see. Fully open, you can take in everything, but light, dust, or foreign objects can easily be damaging. The solution? Moveable eyelids.

With emotions, we have a similar possibility. If we are completely, totally open emotionally expressing every sentiment, we will be open to injury or harm. If we are completely closed, we will be unable to feel or to connect with how others are feeling. Neither is ideal. The solution is emotional regulation.

As an example, you join a meeting feeling the emotion of skepticism. You are poised to disagree or resist what you hear. You are closed. As you listen, you begin to realize that what is being said makes some sense. You get curious. You are opening. By the end of the meeting, you are feeling that you'd like to try out what was taught. You've moved to intrigue and are now fully open. They all may happen without you being aware of it, but it is also something you can learn to do with intention.

Why the split personality? The word itself derives from a Latin root that meant *"to wound, hurt, or maim"*. More generally, it means *"open to attack"*. So, when we choose to be vulnerable, we are opening ourselves to the possibility that others will injure us intentionally or not. What makes vulnerability possible is developing the ability to protect or take care of ourselves when needed.

Regulating vulnerability

It would seem we have three choices:

- Aim for invulnerability, which would require us to be closed to all relationships
- Set ourselves up as completely open, which would allow anyone to hurt us
- Balance our vulnerability with our ability to take care our ourselves

This last option is associated with a powerful list of emotions: Dignity and indignation, respect and self-respect, self-compassion, trust, and self-confidence.

Being more vulnerable can make you more powerful. It allows you to show others who you are and what you care about. Dr. Brené Brown says, "Vulnerability is our most accurate measure of courage. When we shut ourselves off from vulnerability, we distance ourselves from the experiences that bring purpose and meaning to our lives and our work."

Emotions for the journey

There are emotions that can ease your emotional learning journey. Humility, we've already spoken about. Curiosity is essential. A third is perseverance, continuing to look for a way in, a perspective that makes sense to you. Fourth is self-compassion. Give yourself permission to learn at the pace that works for you. Ease up on self-judgment. And, finally, gratitude that you have already been gifted with emotions. You didn't earn them. You didn't get them because you deserve them. They were a gift as part of your humanity. Typically, when we receive a gift, we show respect by opening it and thanking the giver. Maybe it is time.

Questions to ask yourself

- How does this chapter change your perception of these key emotions?
- Which did you know about but weren't sure of their meaning or purpose?
- Which do you believe would benefit you most to focus on?
- Where would you place yourself on the humility-hubris continuum?
- Where would you place yourself on the vulnerability continuum, and is there a shift that might be helpful for you either professionally or personally?
- Are there things you do that, even though important, feel like sacrifice? What possibilities can you imagine to lessen their drain on your energy?

Practical application

- **Personal Growth in Emotional Literacy:**
  - ○ **Seek Feedback:** Open channels of communication with your team. Encourage honest feedback about your leadership style, decision-making, and interpersonal interactions. Asking for feedback is a skill, and trying to read someone's mind is not.
  - ○ **Self-assess:** Regularly evaluate your emotional responses to situations. Understand your self-talk, what ignites you, your strengths, and what you are like when you are stressed/overextended.
  - ○ **Mindfulness Practices:** Dedicate time for mindfulness and meditation, fostering self-awareness and emotional regulation.

Chapter 12
Taking it to the Street

"Nothing is fully learned until it is fully applied".

- Randall K. Murphy

Chapter bullets

- Individual emotional growth is great but won't change the system
- How to begin sharing and cultivating emotional literacy in your agency
- How to spread emotional literacy to your family and community

Story

Leadership is the stewardship of the lives entrusted to you.

It was 5 a.m. on the morning of February 8, 2023. Lieutenant Robert Davison of the Mosaic Park Police Department had proudly served his community for 25 years. But with two ex-wives, an estranged relationship with his daughter, and a tyrannical deputy chief for a boss, Davison was struggling to keep things together. So, at the end of his shift, Davison had made the decision.

Today was the day he was going to commit suicide.

Davison began the day by keeping his usual routine of stopping by the local coffee shop for a triple latte before heading into the station to begin the monotonous tasks of reading and replying to emails. Davison's morning concluded with a brief meeting with his deputy chief, a young man with 10 years less experience but who had excelled at passing civil service promotional exams.

Around lunchtime, Davison shut the door to his office…to reflect on how he arrived at the point of ending it all.

Several memories came to mind.

There was that time when he responded to a woman being physically assaulted by her much bigger and stronger boyfriend. Davison arrived and fought for several minutes until a backup officer could assist. It was one of many days that Davison had feared for his life.

There was that time where he responded to an unconscious 2-year-old and attempted CPR until medics arrived and confirmed that the child was deceased. Davison remembered going home at the end of the shift to his young daughter, waking her up out of a deep sleep to hold her tightly.

There was that time where he responded to a man hanging on the ledge of a bridge of a busy highway, considering jumping to his death. Davison remembered talking to the young man for an hour, begging him not to jump. Now, Davison was in the same situation. This memory brought tears to his eyes because he desperately wanted someone to talk him off the ledge.

A knock came at the door of Davison's office. He wiped the tears from his eyes and answered. Officer Frank Anderson stood there with a young woman in her 20s. Anderson said, "Hey Lt., I need a ride-along form for Lexi Davison. She's interested in becoming a police officer because she grew up watching her dad be a cop for many years and…"

About that time, Davison, Anderson, and Lexi's eyes met. Lexi spoke, "Hey Dad…we haven't talked in a while, but I've wanted to be like you my entire life. I know the job is hard, but I remembered loving all the exciting stories you'd tell me when I was younger. I'm ready to apply and hope to serve as long as you have."

Davison was suddenly filled with emotion. How could he allow his only daughter to go into the same profession that had led him to the point he was at that day?

Davison hugged his daughter and told her he loved her. Davison provided the form to Officer Anderson so Lexi could proceed with her ride-along.

Later that evening, Davison made a different choice by writing a request to his deputy chief asking to be transferred to the Training Division so he could influence others, including his own daughter, on how to navigate the ups and downs of the path of a noble police officer. Davison realized he was a steward.

"Know that leadership is the stewardship of the lives entrusted to you."

Everybody Matters: The Extraordinary Power of Caring for Your People Like Family by Bob Chapman and Raj Sisodia (2017)

Vernell D., Commander

Successive Approximation Collectively Applied

There is a big difference between inspection conversations and learning conversations. Coaching others' performance and development helps ensure that their best day is still out ahead of them. Seniority does not always equal quality. Longevity does not always equal competency.

If you are a leader within your agency, your job is what you get paid to do. Your job is the rank or title you hold within your agency. Your role is something different and may include acting as a coach, advisor, teacher, mentor, or guide.

Providing feedback may be part of your job, but the way you do it reveals which role you see yourself in. Said differently, coaching is not about your position, it is about your disposition.

Five areas of focus that help every first responder grow and enrich life:

1) Start a conversation. True conversation is the linguistic equivalent of exploring the unknown together. You don't need to have the answer to start a conversation, you just need to ask a question.

2) Share your learning and its value. What has it helped you see that you were blind to? What has it helped you do better? Some lessons can be taught, and some lessons have to be learned.

3) Offer teaching. The mantra "learn > do > teach" is full of wisdom. Everyone that you see in your agency is your teacher. Recognize that every person is your teacher, some teaching you what to do and some teaching you what not to do. And we, the Authors, think that one who teaches you what not to do might be just as important as one who teaches you what to do.

When you teach, you always learn, and so do they. Telling is not teaching.

4) Offer coaching. The purpose of coaching is the realization of the complete potential of each member of the team. Coaching is meant to generate new perspectives, which opens unseen possibilities for new and improved actions, and those often lead to better outcomes. Simple, effective, and sustainable.

5) Be an example. From birth, we learn through imitation. We observe, assimilate, imitate, and then attempt behavior based on that of those we believe know things we need to figure out. The vast majority of our social behavior is developed by mimicking others. Everything we do and say with a member of our team has an effect, otherwise, we would be irrelevant. Be someone for them to imitate.

Improving your agency

Think of some of the more controversial events in law enforcement over the last decade. In most of those cases, the officer or officers involved were put in a position they may not have been emotionally prepared for. These events prove that a career in policing is not just physically hazardous; it is also emotionally hazardous. We propose that we've all been looking in the wrong place for an answer. We believe the "reason" is emotional ignorance and illiteracy. And not just with one officer's individual emotions, but the emotions generated in a group of people.

The collective power of emotions is visible in many situations:

- The crowd cheering (or booing) at a football game.
- Wild dancing at a disco
- Solemnity mixed with joy and pride at a graduation ceremony
- Applause as a sign of appreciation at a live art performance
- The collective moments of reflection at a religious service
- Street protests

In each example, identifiable emotions spread through and shape the behavior of the collective. So, what emotions take over a group of officers in a tense situation, and how can emotional practice help avoid the outcomes we witness?

Which collective emotions lead to the difficult-to-comprehend situations we witness? Fear, anger, resentment, fury, rage, and a sense of power that comes from arrogance or hubris are often part of the mix.

What emotions can help defuse a situation like that, and how?

- **Honor** - Choosing to do "the right thing", the morally correct thing, rather than being swayed by what others are doing.

- **Guilt** - When we feel guilt, it is time to reconsider our behaviors because they are surely out of alignment with our values.
- **Dignity** - Acting in accordance with our best self rather than following the crowd. Treating others as our equals.
- **Dispassion** - Being pragmatic and unswayed by the emotions of others. Setting aside passion and acting according to the evidence or facts.
- **Respect** - Treating others as valuable. Listening.
- **Compassion** - Recognizing the struggle of others without the need to fix it or them

These emotions must first be generated in you. They can then be spread to your team to help them release the energy of the causal emotions. Just as an individual must take responsibility for his or her emotions, a team must also. When we don't choose our emotion, it chooses for us.

Culture, Identity, and Image

Culture, identity, and image all play significant roles in policing.

- **Culture** refers to the shared values and behaviors of a group of people, and it can influence how first responders interact with each other, as well as with members of the community.
- **Identity** is the way individuals perceive themselves (their purpose and significance), how they are perceived by others, and it impacts how first responders approach their work and interact with different communities.
- **Image** refers to the way that police departments are perceived by the public, and it can have a significant impact on the perception of needs, motivation, trust, and power between police and the community they serve.

Culture, by nature, is a double-edged sword. Police culture is not different. On the one hand, it can create a sense of unity and purpose among first responders, which can lead to a strong sense of loyalty and camaraderie. On the other hand, police culture can lead to isolation from the community. Healthy culture is the clear water each member of the department drinks every day.

Loyalty is one of the primary emotions that makes culture possible. It is an unusual emotion because there are many possibilities for where loyalty can be focused. Loyalty motivates you to defend your department, your colleagues, your superior, an ideal, a process, your values and beliefs, or the community you serve. When people use the term "conflict of interest," they are often talking about conflicting loyalties. When you say you are loyal, reflect for a moment to whom, to what, and to what degree.

Identity

Identity also plays a significant role in policing. First responders come from a variety of backgrounds and have different perceptions of their role in the community. For example, an officer who sees themselves primarily as a "law and order" enforcer will approach their work differently than an officer who sees themself as a guardian. These different identities can impact how first responders interact with the community and how the community perceives them. Clarity, not just about the identity you have but what identity you want, is part of your journey.

Image

The third leg of the stool, image, is an essential aspect of policing. Police departments rely on the trust and cooperation of the communities they serve, and the image they project can impact that trust. For example, if first responders are perceived as unapproachable or aggressive, members of the community are unlikely to come forward with information or to seek help from the police. Similarly, if police departments are perceived as corrupt or biased, trust is eroded and it is difficult or impossible for the police to effectively do their work.

Each of these three aspects, culture, identity, and image, is shaped by emotions. By building a robust palette of emotions and understanding the way they work, it is possible to choose those that will enhance culture, identity, and image, and those that will undermine them. Identifying and embedding the emotions that generate the agency you envision is your work.

Overall, culture, identity, and image are some of the most critical factors in effective policing. Police departments must do the uncomfortable work to create a culture that promotes safety, respect, equity, inclusion, and belonging. First responders must be mindful of how their individual identities impact their interactions with the community. Finally, police departments must work to project an image to the public that builds and maintains trust and cooperation with the communities they serve.

One of the biggest killers of agency cultural evolution is *contempt prior to investigation*. This can manifest when members of the culture get a sniff that something is evolving in the agency that could lead to working differently. Immediate resistance, rebellion, and polarization begins. Cynicism is in the house.

What gets in the way?

A retired Fire Chief, who defended his Doctor of Liberal Studies dissertation on Culture, Identity, and Image in Fire in 2023, wrote a one-paragraph perspective on how attempts to change fire and police culture, identity, and image are similar. Here is what he shared with us:

"Improving culture is difficult for any organization, perhaps amplified for public safety entities. Behaviors, attitudes, and perceptions may be influenced not only by identity and organizational culture, but also by the persona archetype. According to Carl Jung, the persona archetype can be likened to a series of masks used to project a particular image to a specific audience.

Public safety organizations such as police and fire agencies have institutionalized behaviors, attitudes and perceptions that are difficult to modify, partly because these behaviors, attitudes, and perceptions may have been successful in the past and partly because of ego. Behaviors and attitudes are defended in spite of adaptive attempts to influence the current environment.

Challengers to the existing situation may consequently be discredited or even ridiculed. Challengers are not necessarily those with positional authority but may be any individual with a position counter to the existing identity and culture of the organization. To maintain personal safety, one persona may be given to project an image to colleagues and another to the public that is consistent with the existing culture. Behaviors inconsistent with progressive industry standards may therefore persist."

In other words, as a police chief seeking to evolve your department, you will continually grapple with the intertwined issues of identity, image, and culture. Your department's identity stems from a paramilitary structure and crime-fighting mandate. Externally, frequent media coverage of excessive force and abuse of authority has created an image of the biased and aggressive "bad cop."

As police chief, you must find ways to honor the identity and culture that first responders hold dear while reinventing your image as trusted and just guardians of the community. It is a difficult balance to strike. Evolving the first responders' identity and culture is a gradual process requiring relationship building, transparency, accountability, updated policies, and emphasis on a community caretaking role. As the leader, you must be the catalyst for an identity transformation centered on compassionate public service and protection.

Elevating your agency's culture, identity, and image requires rigorous honesty, openness, and the willingness to look beyond traditional frameworks.

Places that you, as a leader, can begin

Step 1. Start by co-creating a culture of psychological safety. That is a culture where people are confident that they won't be punished or humiliated for speaking up with ideas, questions, concerns, or mistakes. A safe and respectful culture + first responder dignity = increased potential and the probability of the first responder self-reporting when they struggle with their well-being. Equity and inclusion grow out of and from a safe and respectful culture.

Step 2a. Equity is created by ensuring that processes and programs are impartial, fair, and provide equal possible outcomes for every individual. Equity involves trying to understand and give people what they need to enjoy full and healthy lives. Equality, by contrast, aims to ensure that everyone gets the same things with the hope that it will allow them to enjoy full and healthy lives. They are easy to confuse, but the distinction is vital.

Step 2b. Inclusion is felt in an environment that is holistic and recognizes the unique contributions each colleague and their team make to the richness of a diverse culture. Inclusion must be attended to, especially when it is inconvenient or uncomfortable. Belonging and believing grow out of equity and inclusion.

Step 3. Belonging is a felt and lived experience. It results from effectively doing the work of diversity, equity, and inclusion. In addition, the individual must believe they are sincerely invited to belong and choose to accept. Belonging and believing are interdependent. To the degree we feel we belong is to the degree we will be loyal to and believe in the agency. How do you know when you belong? The same way you know when you are hungry. You feel it. It is a felt sense. Belonging is not an intellectual 'get'. Belonging is a behavioral get. I have to behave my way into having others feel that they belong. A possible mindset to bring this about could be that you worry less that people like you and more that people like themselves more when they are around you. That takes more than goodwill, that takes real skill that grows out of your emotional competence.

Step 4. Believing that decisions are made with you and your best interest in mind.

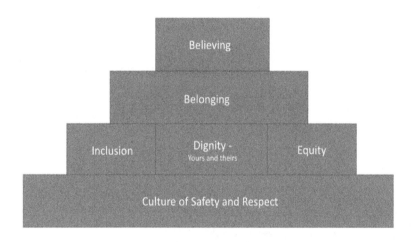

How do you share your learning with your agency?

Non-traditional learning

What we refer to as 'formal education' was a political creation. Napoleon was committed to universal education, but his motivation was not altruism; it was control. He saw it as a way of indoctrinating the masses with the "right" principles, one of them being to keep him as their emperor. Even the way classrooms are organized, the teacher standing in front of rows of students, echoes a military assembly. Although formal education is appropriate and effective in many situations, the majority of our learning happens in non-traditional formats.

Non-traditional techniques

- **Create conversations**

The original Latin meaning of the word conversation was "to go together". A true conversation changes, even if in a small way, the perspective of all participants. We come together with our understanding, and it is expanded. Conversations aren't always verbal. Reading a book is a conversation. Listening to a podcast is as well. Some conversations include another person, but you can have an amazing conversation with yourself. How could you create a conversation about what you've learned in this book? Where would you start? How would you continue? What other ways could you initiate conversations in your agency?

- **Encourage collegial coaching**

As we age, we begin to lose some of our faculties. We can't remember quite as well as we used to. We sometimes get a bit confused. We don't hear as acutely or understand as quickly. A friend of the authors says that it isn't that we become disabled, what is happening is that we were temporarily enabled, but didn't realize it. As children we were unable, we developed and were able for a time, and now we are returning to being unable.

However, even as this is happening, we have a resource that is of significant value, something that keeps us relevant. Wisdom. When is the right time to push ahead? When is it better to wait? When is it more productive to talk? When is listening the best approach? How can letting go be empowering? How can one hold life's challenges in equanimity? How can they best use all the input that is so readily available? These questions cannot be answered with more data. Wisdom is the art side of decision-making and of living well.

Knowledge, information, and data are more available than ever. What many are hungry for is wisdom. Your wisdom can be shared formally or informally through coaching and mentoring.

- **Coaching**

Coaching isn't what we do <u>instead</u> of growing people and impacting results; it is what we do <u>to</u> grow people and impact results. It is a psychologically safe conversation that helps the person being coached see their situation from a new perspective. It requires the coach to be fully present, to listen acutely, and to be unattached to the outcome. What the coachee does with their insights is up to them. They will either change or not change according to the consequences they choose to face. Remember what we shared earlier, as a coach, the biggest shareholder piece you can have in the other person's development is 49%.

Coaching always includes feedback. Observation followed by feeding back to the coachee what you observe. For some, providing feedback can be uncomfortable, which might cause us to hesitate or stand down. Getting used to that discomfort helps create a coaching culture.

But, all feedback presented positively, is positive feedback. As the leader, you are essentially saying, *"I'm interested in your performance and your success, and here are my observations about your performance that could help you succeed." (Acclivus Coaching Model)*

Feedback is positive because of the "way" you present it to the individual. When you forget this, you may be judging, degrading, condescending, criticizing, or punishing, but you are not coaching.

152

Feedback regarding performance deficiency doesn't have to be any less positive than feedback regarding performance proficiency.

At first, everyone is unskilled at coaching. When we learn new things, we are often clumsy. Give yourself permission to be clumsy and sincere when you are providing feedback. The opposite of clumsy and sincere is slick and insincere, and nobody wants that.

Positive Feedback has four important characteristics (BOSS)

- POSITIVE FEEDBACK is **balanced**. You display an equal concern for identifying performance proficiencies, competencies, and deficiencies.
- POSITIVE FEEDBACK is **objective**. You base your feedback to the individual on how they are performing relative to accepted standards for performance.
- POSITIVE FEEDBACK is **specific**. You identify observable and measurable elements of performance, and when recommending a change, you communicate specifically what to change and why.
- POSITIVE FEEDBACK is **supportive**. You present information about performance in a way that communicates your positive expectations and your belief in the individual's ability to succeed.

Our tongue is the dipstick to the heart. When you coach others, guide the conversation in a way that makes the other person feel that you are willing to have this conversation because you care about both of you. Keep the relationship bigger than the problem, and do not treat the person like they are the problem.

Feedback can be appropriate when you notice:

- **Disregard for self or other**s - showing or not showing respect, dignity, acceptance, or compassion.

- **Professional misconduct** - Sarcasm, pre-judging others, taking unwarranted risks, or simple meanness.
- **Lack of effective communication** - not responding to emails, returning calls, sharing information, or helping the other person understand.
- **Unresponsiveness** - ignoring others' requests, not providing appropriate equipment, not taking concerns, or questions to higher levels for answers.
- **Not observing grooming standards** - cleanliness, beards, hair, uniforms, etc.

And you can always share your observations when these things are going well. Studies show that it takes seven positive statements to offset the impact of one negative. From that perspective, you probably will not overdo acknowledgements of behaviors you consider appropriate.

Now, with the advent of new technology – with dash cams, body cameras, and citizen cellphones – everyone has become an expert in policing, and accusations against the police can run rife before cases have been investigated.

In the wake of recent high-profile police-involved incidents, effectively dealing with the challenges of the job has become increasingly difficult. Eighty-six percent of the officers surveyed in 2016 said these incidents have made police work harder than it used to be. Although we have armed our policing professionals with the latest physical protections and tracking equipment, we have yet to completely solve the issue of officers getting emotionally hijacked on the job.

Barbara A Schwartz argues that "our culture fails to acknowledge the realities of emotional suffering" for first responders. "Until the misconceptions are eradicated, stigmas and mental illness labels will remain that stand in the way of officers seeking help." So how can law enforcement leaders address the 21st-century challenges and equip their employees to handle the emotional ups and downs of the job?

One key is emotional literacy, which gives us greater agility, resilience, choice, strength, and understanding. It needs to be learned "offline" so we can use it "online". The moment to learn about rage is not when we are enraged, just as the time to learn about CPR isn't the moment someone is having a heart attack. Learn now so you are better prepared to do later. Practice offline so your emotions are available online.

If we don't elevate our emotional awareness and competence, one and all, how will we even know who is in need of support until it is too late?

Questions to ask yourself

- How are you doing when it comes to coaching others who are different from you?
- If you were to ask others within your agency the difference between working in an environment that is committed to equity or to equality, how many of them would answer correctly?
- How do you feel about your place and role within this department, and are there any experiences or moments that have influenced this feeling?
- If someone makes a mistake in your agency, is it often held against them?
- Are members of your agency able to bring up problems and tough issues?
- Is it safe to take a risk in your agency?
- How difficult is it to ask other members in the agency for help?

- Do you provide clear expectations and consistent feedback, ensuring that every individual you coach understands their roles, responsibilities, and the standards of performance they're held to?

- How natural is it for you to treat every first responder equally regardless of their background or experience level?

- Given the diverse personalities and learning styles of first responders who report to you, are you flexible in your coaching approach to meet them where they need to be met, while still upholding the department's standards?

- Are you effectively emphasizing the importance of safety in all situations, ensuring that first responders not only know the procedures but understand the rationale behind them?

- Do you coach in a way that encourages risk assessment and the use of de-escalation techniques when appropriate?

- Do you coach both the emotional and mental well-being of the first responder, recognizing the strains of the job?

- When others on your team look up and see you creating value in their lives, what are you doing?

Practical application

View your culture as drinking water. Is your agency's drinking water clear and fresh? Everyone is drinking from it on a daily basis.

Assemble an Agency Culture Team:

- Create a dedicated team consisting of colleagues from all backgrounds, experiences, and roles. Obsess on *Celebrating, Recognizing, Appreciating,* and *Protecting* the culture. Many agencies we work with do a good job celebrating, recognizing, and appreciating others within the culture. Agency cultures have to be protected. What is your department's strategy for protecting your culture as it moves forward?

- Consider asking around as to whether or not colleagues feel like they belong or do they feel like they just fit in. When the Chief says, "We are family," do they feel part of the family? Fitting in and belonging are very different. Fitting into a culture often entails adhering to external norms and expectations, whereas a sense of belonging stems from authentic self-expression and mutual respect that fosters an environment where all identities are embraced and valued. Do your recruitment/hiring practices enable candidates to feel they belong?

- Tear down and/or rebuild your existing hiring process if it is cold, generic and out of date. You are not just recruiting first responders; you are building a family. A family that must trust, support, and understand one another. When a candidate feels they belong from the very start, it instills confidence in our department's values, underscores our commitment to unity and inclusivity, and sets the tone for a safe and respectful working environment. Moreover, when first responders feel they belong, they are more likely to remain committed, dedicated, and loyal to the force and the community we serve.

- Retention of current first responders in your profession and understanding of your community's fabric are vital. Prioritizing retention isn't just about numbers; it's about maintaining trust, respect, and a blend of tradition with modern practices. Every retained first responder bridges trust with our citizens and guides newcomers. Your emphasis on retention is a deep commitment to our agency, community, and the essence of service.

- Career planning for first responders who are 10-15 years into their policing career is still so important. Some of these colleagues may feel stuck. They can feel the heat, but they can not see the light. Maybe we should ask them what is currently keeping them in policing. Maybe we should ask them what will keep them in policing next year. We have to help them sometimes to recommit to the commit and help them keep their ability matched in alignment with their responsibility.

Co-Create A Collegial Coaching Program

We offer these five principles for you to use as the basis for training coaches in your agency:

1. Don't assume. Ask.
2. Understand first, then suggest. It works best to keep the horse before the cart.
3. Coaching is more than telling war stories. Share what might help the mentee achieve their goals, solve their challenges, and meet their needs; otherwise, it doesn't need to be said.
4. Coaching is more about building relationship skills than technical competence.
5. Coaching is more about sharing your wisdom more than your knowledge.

The intelligence of a coach can be gauged by their response, but the wisdom of a coach is revealed in their questions. Develop programs that support and coach agency colleagues from all backgrounds.

From resistance to commitment

Techniques to help you move your department from resistance, to compliance, to acceptance, to commitment:

- **Lead with learning:** Link your agency goals/objectives to all learning and development initiatives. If employees see what you are doing as training, then they treat it as training as in basic training, potty training, and remedial training. Training and learning are different. Elevate learning in your agency.

High-impact learning combines 1. clear links to the organization's goals, and 2. individual commitment to the new processes that come from explaining "why us?", "why this?", "why now?".

- **Alignment** can be overlooked as an essential consideration when new skills and strategies are introduced. If they are seen to conflict with (can't use it) or irrelevant to (won't use it) the person or their work they will not stick. Strategize how you can show the value and alignment of emotional development in individual and collective success.
- **Predisposition**: The openness of learners can be strongly influenced by answering some critical questions before they are asked:

  o Why are we doing this?
  o What are we doing?
  o How will it work?
  o If I do this, what's in it for me, the team and the agency?

- **Reinforcement:** Coaching to the new standards and implementation of the new tools and processes. Let's all remember that nothing is fully learned until it is fully applied.
- **Feedback:** Continuous feedback to dial-up/dial-back the predisposition and mood.
- **Tracking Progress:** Link indicators of progress to the specific goals, challenges, and needs of the performance development initiative.
- **Business Review:** The business review with the leaders usually occurs six to twelve months after the initial working session. It typically leads back to the assessment phase.

Chapter 13
Dignity, the Über Emotion

"I have often wondered how it is that every man loves himself more than all the rest of men, but yet sets less value on his own opinions of himself than on the opinions of others."

\- Marcus Aurelius

Chapter bullets:

- What makes dignity the new empathy
- The many faces of dignity
- When dignity is threatened

Story

I sat in the airport and watched the news. It was 2:30 AM, and my partner and I were about to board a one-direction flight across the country to attempt to locate two missing persons who we feared were already gone. The story was about a family who had been looking for their missing child for 20 years. My partner and I looked at each other, and we knew. This was not going to be easy; this was going to burn its scar into us and we needed to do it with courage, integrity, within the boundaries of the law, and ensure that we did our job as officers and investigators. We knew the price if we didn't. We were watching it.

Fast forward five years later. Three months after a capital murder trial, the missing couple had been located across the country states away from where the suspect had been located and interviewed, and we got a guilty, not only a guilty but a death. In that instant, I wasn't pleased with my work or happy for the families involved – my exact thoughts were, "I now understand why major case investigators leave soon after a once-in-a-lifetime case is done."

My reality was I had depleted my emotional gauge and was disconnected from the world at that moment. I was heartbroken and lost. I had become the job, and this case was what had defined me for half of my career. I needed a change like so many of my colleagues before me. It was hard, it was painful, and it was sometimes misunderstood. I mourned the person I was when I got that case and had to learn who I was now. I didn't want to be jaded, or stone. I had to understand that my emotions helped guide me. I had to look in the mirror and find out what I was made of – I didn't need the job, the job needed me.

It was going to be hard and it's a struggle daily to make sure I remain open to that vulnerability. Some days, the work is harder than others, but most days, I know why I want to stay the course, and I commit to a better me. A better me for myself, my family, my coworkers, and my future self.

Ashley C., Detective

We began this book by stating that our goal was to "prioritize dignity in policing." Since then, we've used the word dignity 105 times. We'd like to conclude by sharing why we believe dignity is the über emotion when it comes to your life as a first responder.

The simplest place to begin is with its original meaning in Latin, "worthy". The belief that we have inherent worth as human beings can be traced back to the book of Genesis and the creation story, and it has been repeated by every generation of thinkers, writers, athletes, leaders, and workers since.

"Dignity means a belief in oneself, that one is worthy of the best. It means that I deserve the best treatment I can receive. And that I have the responsibility to give the best treatment I can to other people."

- Maya Angelou

When we feel the emotion of dignity, it imbues us with the certainty that we are of value no matter our successes or failures. It is the one thing we have as human beings that no one can take away from us.

"Any man who tries to rob me of my dignity will lose."

- Nelson Mandela

One litmus test for dignity is to ask yourself, "Does this work for me?". Things that don't are often clashing with your dignity. This can happen when someone speaks to you, speaks about you, or treats you in a way that does not acknowledge your value as a human being. The issue isn't that they are wrong, but that they are crossing a boundary you have set for yourself. They may not know where the boundary is, and sometimes you may not be sure either, but you will feel when it is crossed, and when you do, you can take a stand for yourself.

"One's dignity may be assaulted, vandalized and cruelly mocked, but cannot be taken away unless it is surrendered."

- Michael J. Fox

But taking a stand for yourself does not mean attacking the other person. It can come as a simple "No". It can come as a request. You can ignore the incident for the moment and choose to have a conversation later in private. There are many ways to take a stand for what you believe, but taking a stand from dignity includes extending dignity to the other person as part of the deal.

"Human dignity is the same for all human beings; when I trample on the dignity of another, I am trampling on my own."

- Pope Francis

Dignity is not about what we do, but who we are. All of our actions originate there which means that when we believe we have worth it translates into everything we do. It shows up in the way we walk, talk, listen, work, play, and relate.

"Remember this - that there is a proper dignity and proportion to be observed in the performance of every act of life."

- Marcus Aurelius

It applies equally no matter our gender.

"A woman's dignity is not dependent on the approval of others, but on her own self-respect and worth."

Unknown

No matter our race.

"The basic tenet of black consciousness is that the black man must reject all value systems that seek to make him a foreigner in the country of his birth and reduce his basic human dignity."

- Steve Biko

And, it is a gift.

"The most luxurious possession, the richest treasure anybody has, is his personal dignity." - Jackie Robinson.

It is at the core of how we treat others.

"Sweetest Lord, make me appreciative of the dignity of my high vocation, and its many responsibilities. Never permit me to disgrace it by giving way to coldness, unkindness, or impatience."

- Mother Teresa

"There is a healthful hardiness about real dignity that never dreads contact and communion with others, however humble".

- Washington Irving

It is a choice.

"Relationships based on obligation lack dignity".

- Wayne Dyer

There is little of more importance in life.

"When it comes to human dignity, we cannot make compromises."

- Angela Merkel

Dignity…

- Challenges us to take responsibility for our emotions. *("The ability to respond")*
- Gives us the power to set personal boundaries *(how do we want to be treated? How close is too close?)*
- Clarifies what we need (*respect, consideration, support*)
- Reveals to us what we want (*without regard to what others want first*)
- Gives us the choice to speak or remain quiet as we believe best
- Empowers us to choose for us
- Gives us access to indignation to protect our personal boundaries *(to say 'no')*
- Gives us the grounding to apologize and forgive

164

- Allows us access to all the other emotions
- Frees us from shame, guilt, and embarrassment
- Is a channel for us to connect with and elevate others
- Brings us inner peace
- Lets us move through life with strength, courage, and safety
- Helps us stop people-pleasing, creating unmet expectations, and resentments.
- Eliminates the need to compare ourselves to others
- Assures we live the best version of ourselves
- Allows us to affirm ourselves rather than looking to others for affirmation

We do these things for others all of the time. Who does them for us?

The target

The aim of intellectual development is that we can choose how we think. We can decide where we will apply our thinking to make a difference. The aim of emotional development is that we can choose how we emote. We can put our emotions to work for us rather than fighting with them.

The authors see the most important outcome of emotional learning to be emotional regulation. That means using emotions as a tool to raise or lower our energy, move closer or farther away in relationships, to step into the future, or reflect on the lessons of the past. Emotional regulation is possible when we acknowledge that we have native emotional intelligence, we build our emotional literacy, and practice emotional resilience and agility. Emotional mastery emerges as we increase our ability to understand and regulate our emotions when and as we choose.

©2023 Dan Newby and Marcel Brunel

If you take even small steps in these four you will end up being able to regulate one of the most important tools imaginable: your emotions.

Changing the "visible" - friends, food, clothes - seems to be easier than changing the invisible - our thoughts and emotions. But there is a reason why interior growth and change are essential and rewarding. In every forest, on every farm, in every orchard on earth, what is underground creates what is above ground. You cannot change the fruits that are already hanging on the tree. You can, however, change tomorrow's. But to do so, you will have to dig below the ground and nurture the roots. It is worth the effort because when you succeed at evolving, it ensures the best day you will ever have is one that is still out ahead of you.

You are at the part of your transformational journey where discomfort is necessary. Deep, lasting change requires accessing your insecurities and fears and facing them. This is, by nature, uncomfortable. And you can do it.

At the beginning of the book, we shared that we wrote this book to say something about emotional literacy and, particularly, dignity in policing. If we have said something you believe is incorrect or incomplete, let us know. Please charge the mistake to our heads and not our hearts.

With gratitude and anticipation,

Dan and Marcel

FAQs

Below, we've shared some of the questions we are most often asked about emotional literacy. If you have a question that is not addressed, please contact us directly, and we will respond to your query. Marcel Brunel and Dan Newby can be contacted through LinkedIn or by email at info@dignityinpolicing.com.

Q: If the emotion of dignity helps keep the profession of policing a noble one, what emotion depletes its standing?

A: There are several, including resentment, hubris, greed, and disrespect, but the strongest is probably entitlement. When we believe "the world owes us". When, for no reason we can name, we believe we deserve a certain role, income, privileges, relationships, or other things in life. The world owes us nothing but often gives us many gifts.

Q: Does expanding emotional literacy increase emotional intelligence?

Short answer: Yes, you can substantiate a correlation between increased emotional literacy (expanded vocabulary, etc.) and Emotional Intelligence as assessed by an instrument.

Long answer: I think this question falls under the "know about/know how" umbrella. An EI assessment helps the individual **know about** themselves. Their blind spots. What they might want to dial up or dial back in their personality. Emotional literacy comes next and helps the individual then **know how** to maybe become more compassionate, bold, or courageous.

Emotional literacy refers to an individual's ability to understand, express, and navigate their emotions effectively. It involves having a rich vocabulary to describe emotions, recognizing, and interpreting emotional cues in oneself and others, and being able to regulate emotions in different situations. EI, on the other hand, is a broader construct that encompasses the ability to perceive, understand, and navigate both one's own emotions and the emotions of others. It involves skills such as self-awareness, self-regulation, empathy, and social skills.

Research has indicated a positive correlation between emotional literacy and emotional intelligence. When individuals possess an expanded emotional vocabulary and have a better understanding of their emotions, they are more likely to exhibit higher levels of emotional intelligence.

Here are a few reasons why this correlation exists:

1) **Vocabulary and Emotional Identification:** Emotional literacy involves having a diverse range of words to describe emotions (your painting palette). By possessing an expanded emotional vocabulary, individuals can more accurately recognize, name, and express their emotions. This enhanced ability to recognize and differentiate emotions is a fundamental aspect of emotional intelligence. Change is an inside job. I cannot improve what I cannot see. Assessments help me see the invisible inside that is causing the visible on the outside. Said differently: My inner game creates my outer game.

2) **Emotional Expression and Regulation:** A rich emotional vocabulary allows individuals to express their emotions more precisely and effectively. When individuals can articulate their emotions, they are better equipped to communicate their feelings to others, which fosters better emotional regulation. This ability to express and regulate emotions is an important component of Emotional Intelligence.

3) **Empathy and Social Skills:** Emotional literacy enhances empathy, which is the ability to understand and share the emotions of others. When individuals have a wider range of emotional words and can accurately perceive emotions in others, they are more likely to exhibit empathic behavior. Empathy is a crucial aspect of EI and plays a significant role in developing and maintaining positive social relationships.

Instruments that assess emotional intelligence, such as self-report questionnaires or performance-based assessments, often include items that tap into an individual's emotional vocabulary and understanding. These assessments aim to capture an individual's ability to recognize and manage emotions effectively. Therefore, individuals with increased emotional literacy are likely to perform better on these instruments, indicating a positive correlation between emotional literacy and assessed emotional intelligence.

It is important to note that emotional intelligence is a multifaceted construct, and emotional literacy is just one component of it. Other factors, such as self-awareness, emotional regulation, and social skills, also contribute to overall emotional intelligence. However, an expanded emotional vocabulary and increased emotional literacy can serve as a foundation for developing and enhancing other aspects of emotional intelligence.

Self-Awareness + Others-Awareness = Intentionality/How you show up. More emotional literacy begets more emotional intelligence...more begets more.

Q: Is a feeling the same as an emotion?

A: A feeling is a sensation. Sometimes it is associated with an emotion, and sometimes it is not. When you feel hunger, it is telling you that your body needs something. If you don't take care of the need, it may provoke an emotion, but the feeling itself is not initially related to an emotion. There are other feelings that are part of or that point to an emotion. When you feel a knot in your stomach, it may be because you are experiencing anxiety. Emotions include sensations or feelings, but also a narrative or story, and impulse.

Q: How is emotional literacy helpful if one is already considered "too emotional"?

A: People are born with different levels of emotional sensitivity. Just as our eyesight is affected by bright light, and our sense of smell, and hearing varies. In the case of sensitive eyes, we may simply adopt wearing sunglasses if the level of light is uncomfortable.

What is unique about being told we are too emotional is that the assessment is generally made by others, so it is not unusual to be labeled in this way because of another person's discomfort.

What emotional literacy helps us do is regulate our emotions. When we understand what is happening within us emotionally, it allows us to make choices about changing our environment, pausing our response, or choosing which emotion will be most useful. When we are emotionally illiterate, we are more prone to believe that "we are our emotions" rather than "we have emotions". That makes a significant difference in our ability to use our emotions as a life skill.

Q: How can I coach someone to help them better develop their emotional literacy?

A: The first question we ask our clients is whether they see value in developing their emotional competence. If not, there is no way to support them. If they say they are interested, the first step is to help them develop the practice of pausing to notice what they are feeling and thinking. The second step is for them to put a name on that experience. What emotion is connected with what they are feeling and thinking? The third is to introduce the concept of navigating emotions. Is the emotion they are in serving them? Is it helping them, or is it a barrier, given their situation? We always have a choice, but don't always recognize that we do. The more one practices these three steps - notice, name, and navigate - the greater one's emotional competence becomes.

Q: How does emotional literacy affect mental wellness?

A: When you are better at noticing, naming, and navigating your emotions, it increases your competence in decision-making, problem-solving, and relationship-building. Emotional literacy also plays a role in helping a first responder to recover from or adjust to challenging situations. This can reduce the risk of burnout and mental health issues like anxiety and depression.

When you are without emotional literacy to help you understand what you are experiencing, you may resort to negative coping mechanisms like substance abuse or aggression. Decades of psychological research show that life satisfaction and internal balance, in the face of traumatic experiences, is less about how many we have experienced and more about how we have navigated them.

Q: What role does emotional literacy play in relationships?

A: One of the primary roles of emotions is allowing us to build and maintain relationships. The relationship we have with ourselves is built on emotions such as dignity, pride, guilt, and acceptance. Relationships with others include another set of emotions: affection, trust, admiration, and compassion. We also have relationships with what is beyond human. Awe, faith, and wonder are part of those relationships. Without emotions, we would be unable to have relationships of any kind.

Q: Can emotional literacy help with anger management?

A: Absolutely! Understanding what anger is telling us is an important first step. The message of anger is that I believe that what

I'm experiencing is unjust or morally wrong. It may not be unjust, but that is what I believe. Understanding that opens the door to consider how we are evaluating our experience. If, on reflection, we do believe the situation is unjust, anger can help us formulate a path to creating more justice. Being able to name anger, or any emotion, changes our relationship with it. It gives us a handle on what is happening, which is an entry point to managing or navigating the emotion.

Q: How does emotional literacy contribute to effective leadership?

A: Leaders are immersed in a sea of emotions - their own and those of their team, their stakeholders, clients, and the public. When we don't understand emotions, it is as if unseen and unnamed forces are acting on all that is happening. That can create confusion and reactive decisions that are not helpful.

If we consider the domain of energy in leadership, it is obvious that a leader's energy is important. It is what helps them engage and accomplish, but it is also transmitted to and affects their followers. If a leader isn't clear on how to select the emotions that will produce an optimal level of energy for them and their team, they are missing a key leadership tool.

Appendix A

Emotions List

Acceptance	Admiration	Adoration
Adventurousness	Affection	Aggravation
Agony	Amazement	Ambition
Amusement	Anger	Anguish
Annoyance	Anticipation	Anxiety
Apathy	Appreciation	Apprehension
Arrogance	Astonishment	Attraction
Awe	Bliss	Boldness
Boredom	Calmness	Care
Certainty	Compassion	Confidence
Confusion	Contempt	Courage
Curiosity	Cynicism	Delight
Denial	Desire	Despair
Dignity	Disappointment	Disgust
Dislike	Dismay	Dispassion
Dissatisfaction	Doubt	Dread
Ease	Ecstasy	Elation
Embarrassment	Empathy	Enthusiasm
Entitlement	Envy	Equanimity
Eroticism	Euphoria	Excitement
Exhilaration	Expectant	Exuberance
Fear	Frustration	Fury
Generosity	Gratitude	Greed
Guilt	Happiness	Hate
Hilarity	Honor	Hope
Hopelessness	Horror	Hubris
Humility	Impatience	Incredulity
Indifference	Indignation	Infatuation
Inspiration	Intrigue	Irreverence

Jealousy	Joy	Kindness
Lasciviousness	Laziness	Lividity
Loneliness	Love	Loyalty
Lust	Magnanimity	Melancholy
Mischievousness	Misery	Modesty
Mortification	Naiveté	Nostalgia
Obligation	Optimism	Panic
Paranoia	Passion	Peace
Perseverance	Pessimism	Pity
Pride	Prudence	Rage
Rebelliousness	Regret	Remorse
Resentment	Resignation	Respect
Reverence	Revulsion	Righteousness
Sadness	Satisfaction	Scorn
Sentimentality	Serenity	Shame
Shyness	Skepticism	Solitude
Stubborn	Surprise	Sympathy
Tenderness	Terror	Thankfulness
Timidity	Tolerance	Triviality
Trust	Uncertainty	Vengeance
Wistfulness	Wonder	Yearning
Zeal		

Acknowledgments:

This book would not have been possible without the contributions of many people. Each person who reviewed our ideas put something of themselves into the manuscript. In addition, they generously shared their stories, experiences, strength, and hope. We are grateful for their interest and support.

Greg Beale, Judi Bargman, Curtis Howard, Amber Stanford, Marc Shimmick, Mike Mowery, Chase Stapp, Bob Miljenovich, Jim Parrish, Danny Barton, Eleanor James, Gerald Hodges, Mark Spaniol, Jeremy Spence, Jim Palma, Dustin Schellenger, Jonathan Aronie, Steve Dye, Adrienne Brunel, Sean Beatty, Jonah Brunel, Stan Standridge, Corina Hicks, Timothy Vaughan, Natalie Nguyen, Bill Snell, Brandy Kidwell, Maurice Brunel, Lisa Martin, Neal Barron, Juan Balderrama, James Groom, Jackie Seabrook, Rick Randall, Brad Fortune, Ashley Cunningham, Lisa Ross, Sarah Keith, David Beckwith, Max Tolliver, Lindsay Waychoff, Danny Kistner, Sam Garrison, Vernal Dooley, Richard Williams, Jared Lemoine, Kary Shaffer, Jalen Rivera, Walter Largent, Dwayne Dean, Ethan Tanner, Sammy Lujan, John Rebman, Eric Louderback, Kenneth Cochran, Juan Ovalle, Kellen Peters, Rick Riley, Bill McManus, Jonathon Kreisner.